Grace Helen Mowat and
the Making of Cottage Craft

Grace Helen Mowat. Courtesy of the Charlotte County Archives

Grace Helen Mowat

and the making of

Cottage Craft

DIANA REES
with Ronald Rees

GOOSE LANE

Edited by Susanne Alexander and Lisa Alward.
Cover and interior page design by Julie Scriver.
Cover photos courtesy of Charlotte County Archives and Matthew Rees.
Printed in Canada.
10 9 8 7 6 5 4 3 2 1

Library and Archives Canada Cataloguing in Publication

Rees, Diana, 1939-2007
Grace Helen Mowat and the making of Cottage Craft / Diana Rees with Ronald Rees.

Includes index.
ISBN 978-0-86492-532-9

1. Mowat, Grace Helen, 1875-1964. 2. Cottage Craft (Firm). 3. Knitting shops — New Brunswick — Saint Andrews. 4. Arts and crafts movement — Canada — History. I. Rees, Ronald, 1935- II. Title.
NK842.N38R44 2009   746.43'0971533   C2008-907199-9

Goose Lane Editions acknowledges the financial support of the Canada Council for the Arts, the Government of Canada through the Book Publishing Industry Development Program (BPIDP), and the New Brunswick Department of Wellness, Culture, and Sport for its publishing activities.

Goose Lane Editions
Suite 330, 500 Beaverbrook Court
Fredericton, New Brunswick
CANADA E3B 5X4
www.gooselane.com

*This book is dedicated to the people of
St. Andrews and Charlotte County.*

Contents

Foreword

Diana Rees came to St. Andrews from Saskatchewan in 1983 to own and operate the Sea Captain's Loft, a store that sold, among other things, British woollens. She had been a librarian, but textiles and design were her first love. Below the Sea Captain's Loft, on the immediate waterfront, was Cottage Craft, another store selling woollens, these supplied by local knitters, weavers, and embroiderers from Charlotte County. The business had been founded seventy years earlier by Grace Helen Mowat, a St. Andrews woman who, approaching mid-life, had also changed careers. Grace Helen had been a reluctant teacher who came home after more than a decade away.

After her retirement, Diana embarked on a biography of Nell Mowat (as she was known to friends and family) and a history of the cottage industry she founded. Her chief sources were Grace Helen Mowat's correspondence and the recollections of people who had known her and her successors in the business, Bill and Kent Ross, or who had worked for Cottage Craft. Before completing the manuscript, however, Diana contracted a disabling and incurable disease. Guided by her, I wrote the final chapters. But this is Diana's book; it was her conception, her research, and, except for some of the words, her writing. I tried to maintain her voice and her attention to detail, and where I failed, Lisa Alward, a skilled and sensitive editor, conducted repairs.

Had Diana lived to see the publication of her book, she would have acknowledged each of her many informants, and all those who generously made available material that she could photograph and use for illustration. Although she made notes on her interviews, and on the handcrafts and artwork in the houses and institutions she visited, inevitably some of the details died with her. To avoid the possibility of overlooking anyone who might have assisted Diana, I did not attempt a list. Those of you who helped her know who you are, and, having met her, you will know how much she appreciated your generosity. Thank you all.

— Ronald Rees

Cottage Craft today, St. Andrews, New Brunswick. Courtesy of Matthew Rees

Introduction

Following his first and only visit to St. Andrews in 1923, the celebrated Canadian poet and author Bliss Carman addressed Grace Helen Mowat in a letter as "My dear Countess of Charlotte." They were longtime friends, but Carman, who lived in Connecticut, had never visited Charlotte County and had no conception of what a prominent figure Nell Mowat really was — not just in the county but throughout New Brunswick. He knew her as a talented but minor poet of regional verse, and as a writer of engaging letters, but her great achievement at the time of his visit was to have founded one of the most successful cottage industries in North America: Charlotte County Cottage Craft.

After a fitful career teaching art in New England and Nova Scotia, Grace Helen Mowat returned home to the Mowat family farm, Beech Hill in St. Andrews, where, as a single woman in her early thirties, with very little capital, she launched her cottage industry in 1913. Using wool from Charlotte County farms that she coloured with vegetable dyes at Beech Hill and had spun into yarn at a local mill, she began supplying weavers and embroiderers throughout the county with material from which to make blankets, bedspreads, bags, woven yard goods, and hooked and woven rugs. For items requiring a motif or pattern, her instructions were simple but firm: look around you and weave, hook, or embroider the colours, scenes, and activities that you see. Her objective was to tell the story of her place and her people; to reproduce in handmade woollen goods the colours, the contours and the life of Charlotte County and New Brunswick. She allowed nothing from catalogues and pattern books, and few raw materials that were not indigenous.

Although she was schooled in the applied and decorative arts in London and New York, Nell Mowat's aims were not narrowly aesthetic. At the very practical Woman's Art School of the Cooper Union in New York, she learned that art must pay. The approval of sophisticated urban buyers and of her peers in the arts and crafts world was important to her, but her overriding objectives were social and economic. As well as making a living for herself, she wanted to improve life for farm families in Charlotte County. Handcrafts, she stated plainly, were a cash crop, as important as oats or barley, that drew on the skills accumulated by generations of farm women. Sold through retail outlets in St. Andrews, and by mail order, her hand-crafts injected cash into a rural economy that was chronically short of it. So determined was Nell to prevent the drift away from the farms that for a decade she badgered the Colonization and Development Department of the Canadian Pacific Railway in Montreal, and the Dominion Department of Agriculture in Ottawa, to provide the seed, equipment, and expert knowledge to initiate and support the growth of flax in the county. Some of this flax fibre would have been spun and woven by her craft workers but her main motive was to provide Charlotte County farmers with a cash crop. She also tried valiantly, but ultimately failed, to found a pottery using clays from the district that would have employed youth in and around St. Andrews.

In her middle years, with Cottage Craft well established, she turned to writing. She produced a book of children's poems that drew high praise from the Canadian writer Sir Charles G.D. Roberts as well as Bliss Carman. She also wrote an unashamedly romantic and, in terms of its effect upon popular perceptions of the town, influential history of St. Andrews. In retirement, she wrote a novel that became the maiden publication of the University Press of New Brunswick in

1951. That same year, nominated by Sir James Dunn, and backed by Lord Beaverbrook, she was awarded an honorary Doctor of Laws by the University of New Brunswick.

As visitors to St. Andrews know, Cottage Craft continues to attract loyal customers. In 1945, Grace Helen Mowat entrusted the business to Kent and Bill Ross, sons of a former student and good friend. Kent and Bill were succeeded, in turn, by Kent's sons, first Jim and then Evan, the current proprietor and manager. The shop, a converted lobster plant that on windy days in summer is skirted by dancing skeins of coloured wool, tied to a low fence of nautical rope and cork floats, perches above the shore in St. Andrews's waterfront market square. It isn't the same shop that Nell Mowat made and, with tide and time and changing tastes, the products have altered somewhat, but her spirit inhabits it.

Most biographies depend on the keeping and safe storage of written records. Following the practice of her family, Nell kept every letter that was ever written to her and to these she added those saved by her parents and grandparents. There is some evidence that Nell culled some of the letters that were not flattering to her — she was not without ego or enemies — but when she died in 1964 she left a treasure trove of letters and papers. In 1979, these letters, and, later, letters written by her aunt Helen to her aunt Susan Mowat in San Francisco, were acquired by the volunteer founders of the Charlotte County Archives in St. Andrews. Duly accessioned, catalogued and microfilmed they are a prized and invaluable collection, spanning most of the first two centuries of the town's history.

Editor's note: While Grace Helen Mowat was a lively writer, her grammar and spelling were often quite loose when hurried. To make the quotations from her letters more readable, light punctuation has been added.

Colonel David Mowat, Grace Helen Mowat's grandfather, circa 1855.

Courtesy of the Charlotte County Archives

"Always Room For One More"

I can fancy dear little Nellie roaming about in her Father's
"domain" by herself & as there are no venomous reptiles
to hurt or molest her, she may, I suppose be left to enjoy
her solitary rambles among the woods & wildflowers . . .
    — Letter from Eliza Parker to Isabella Mowat
    (June 9, 1804)

When Eliza Parker wrote this affectionate vignette to her niece Bella
in 1884, she left a telling portrait of her great-niece, nine-year-old
Grace Helen Mowat. During her "solitary rambles," Grace Helen,
familiarly called Nell or Nellie for most her life, was sending her
own roots down among those of the trees and wildflowers on her
father's farm. As an art student and teacher, she would live away for
many years, but Beech Hill, just outside St. Andrews in the south west
corner of New Brunswick, was her only true home. The farm, town,
and surrounding countryside, were the setting and the support for her
main venture in life: Cottage Craft. The subjects, patterns, and motifs
for her locally made crafts were all drawn from the farms, fields, and
villages of Charlotte County, a milieu so deeply important to her that
she could not have settled in any other place.

Nell was a much-wanted only child, born on January 31, 1875,
when her father, George, was forty-nine and her mother, Isabella
Campbell Mowat, forty-three, but it is unlikely that she was ever
a spoiled one. She came into a busy farm household that already
sheltered three generations. Her grandfather, Colonel David John
Mowat, then eighty, was enjoying retirement on a farm he had helped
clear in his youth, and which was now being worked by George, his
eldest son. Only two years before, the last two of the Colonel's seven

daughters, Bessie and Susan, had left the family home for marriage or employment. One of his two other sons, David Wyer Mowat, had moved to Michigan — which still had large trees — where he could continue to work in the lumber industry. The remaining son, Charles Edward Mowat, had recently acquired his own farm at Bayside on the St. Croix River, a few miles above St. Andrews.

When Nell arrived, her mother, Bella, was also caring for her invalid brother-in-law, Arthur Julian, the husband of her sister Grace Campbell Julian, who had died in 1869, and for the Julian's daughter Ethel, aged eleven. Grace Julian must have been the victim of a lingering illness because Ethel, according to a letter from Nell's Aunt Helen to Susan Mowat, had been Bella's charge "ever since she was born" and had lived at Beech Hill since her mother's death. She was, in effect, an older sister ready and waiting for baby Nell who, when Ethel's father died two and a half months later in April 1875, was probably the source of some consolation and distraction.

The land that would become Beech Hill farm belonged to Nell's great-grandfather, Captain David Mowat. Captain Mowat was a sailing master for the merchants William and Robert Pagan at the time of the founding of St. Andrews in 1783, and like them, he was one of the original land grantees of the Loyalist settlement. On the town plot granted to him, on Water Street, he built a large house (subsequently an inn) where he and his wife Mehetible Calef Mowat lived with their eleven children. In addition to the Water Street lot, he purchased some forested land about a mile north of the town. Captain David died at sea in 1810, and not long afterwards came the political unrest that led to the War of 1812 between the United States and Canada. Mehetible had experienced similar unrest when, as a child of Loyalists, she fled with her mother from Ipswich, Massachusetts, to safe British territory in the Bay of Fundy. In 1812, she needed no persuading to move away from the exposed shore to the forested land her husband had bought some years previously. Her older sons had already cleared some of the land and built a barn, and on the crest of the sloping ground that gave onto Passamaquoddy Bay, they built a solid farmhouse that would be occupied by Mowats for the next 150 years.

Nell and her father, George Mowat, circa 1890.
Courtesy of the Charlotte County Archives

By the standards of the time and place, Beech Hill's one hundred
and fifty acres provided a modest living. Its soils, like those of the
rest of region, were thin and stoney and most suited to pasture for
livestock; by 1871, four years before Nell was born, on hundred
acres had been cleared for pasture, and twenty-five acres mown for
hay. The cereal crops were barley and oats and these, combined
with pasture and hay, supported three driving and work horses,
eight milk cows, six beef cattle, and sixteen sheep. A field crop peculiar to the region was turnips; the farm produced 180 bushels of
them that year, some of which would have been stored for feeding cattle, and the rest shipped from a wharf at nearby Chamcook
and sold for cash in the Boston market. (Turnips were one of the
few non-perishable vegetables in the days before refrigeration.)

Adjacent to the house at Beech Hill was a vegetable garden and orchard, an acre plot of potatoes, a pigpen, and a dozen beehives. Bella Mowat kept chickens and geese, and she regularly sold eggs, a steady if small source of cash. In 1871, according to the Dominion Census, she also churned 600 pounds of butter, while George collected 120 pounds of honey from the hives, sheared 100 pounds of wool, and cut twenty cords of firewood. Nobody went hungry at Beech Hill, but as on any small Maritime farm, actual cash was never plentiful. When younger members of the family went away to work they sent money home if they could spare it, or they saved and paid for large purchases such as a new tailored suit for their father, an overcoat for brother George, or a sewing machine for sister Susan before she herself went away to work.

An additional source of cash at Beech Hill were the summer vacationers who boarded with the Mowats. City folk relished wholesome farm fare and the cool, clean air of Passamaquoddy Bay. While Nell was still an infant, a regular visitor to Beech Hill was Mrs. Weldon, wife of a Fredericton judge. One year, after returning home in late August, she wrote to Bella, "The first greeting here was *the smell of drains.* You who are so accustomed to your fresh sea air have little idea of the stuffiness of inland places. I am not nearly so well & each day am obliged to drop something of the scrumptious fare I indulged in with you... Thanking you much for your great kindness to me & for the most charming days I spent in your happy home." Mrs. Weldon's comments tell us something of the cheerful atmosphere at Beech Hill and help to explain the development of St. Andrews as a resort. In summer, the Bay of Fundy whose massive tides constantly bring up cold water from the ocean depths, is a giant air conditioner that at the turn of the twentieth century drew visitors from the stifling cities of eastern Canada and the eastern seaboard of the United States. The summer influx to St. Andrews, a pattern familiar to Nell from her earliest years, was to have a major bearing on the course of her later life. The immediate effect, however, was that she was showered with many "kisses for Baby" in letters thanking the Mowats for their hospitality. One year, when her husband, the judge, came to preside over the county court in St. Andrews, Mrs. Weldon even found room

Tea party at Beech Hill. Courtesy of the Charlotte County Archives

among his legal paraphernalia for the fabric and a pattern for a dress for young Nell.

An old Scottish nursery tale tells of hospitable Lachie MacLachlan and his wife and ten bairns who, during a storm, offer shelter to all who pass by their rural house: "Och, come away in! There's room galore. Always room for one more!" However numerous the summer visitors, there was "always room for one more" in the generous Mowat household. Aunts, uncles, and cousins, of whom Nell had a great many on both the Mowat and Campbell sides of her family, sometimes visited for the last two or three weeks of summer and were somehow squeezed in. In October 1885, the resident family group was suddenly expanded after George Mowat's forty-five-year-old brother Charles drowned in a sailboat accident on the St. Croix River, within sight of his Bayside farm (now the historic site lookout point for St. Croix Island.)

Charles Mowat had set out to cross the river one windy morning in a recently purchased boat, failing to heed warnings that she was "crank" and needed a lot of ballast. He made the sheet fast and as soon as the boat edged away from the shelter of the land, the wind struck the sail and capsized her. He stayed with the boat for some minutes, shouting and waving his hat, but he succumbed to the deadly cold water before help could reach him. Charles's young widow, Helen, and their three small children came immediately to live at Beech Hill farm: "George and Bella are most kind and insist on their going to them for the winter anyway. It will be so much nicer than going among strangers for Helen, & they are both so kind to the widows and fatherless," wrote Helen's sister to Charles's sister Susan in San Francisco, three days after his death. Ten-year-old Nell now had three more cousins-cum-siblings: Brydone, aged three; Miriam, almost one; and Cuthbert, just two months old. The enlarged family group became a permanent fixture. George Mowat, now aged fifty-nine, and the children grew increasingly fond of one another, as did Bella and the widowed Helen. Several years later, after George had gone out with the horses and sleigh to meet her as she walked home from town in a heavy snow, Helen wrote to Susan, "Oh the dear Brother [George] and Bella are so loving and tender and careful of us all." Not until 1905, when her children were grown and launched into the world, did Helen move into St. Andrews and re-establish a home of her own. Her own sister, Rosa Jack, ("the lively and useful Miss Rosa," as Colonel David Mowat spoke of her in a letter to his daughter Susan) was also often at Beech Hill in the first few years to comfort Helen and help with the children.

To ease the pressure when the Beech Hill seams were close to bursting, a log cabin was built as sleeping quarters for some of the hardier summer boarders. One of these was G.C. Thompson, an Ontario barrister, who, the *St. Andrews Bay Pilot* reported in October 1887, had recently had the misfortune to shoot off the big toe of his right foot "whilst on a gunning expedition" near Hamilton. That summer Thomson spent many weeks with the Mowats. So popular was Beech Hill that in several of the June 1888 issues of the *Bay Pilot*

Early drawing by Nell. Courtesy of the Charlotte County Archives

Bella Mowat advertised for "a good cook," promising the "highest wages" for a satisfactory person.

No record of Nell's early schooling has come to light. Free tax-supported public schools were established in St. Andrews in 1872 and 1873, following the passage of the New Brunswick Schools Act in 1871, but attendance was not compulsory until 1906. At least one private school for younger children seems to have continued for some time after 1873; Nell's uncle, David Wyer Mowat, wrote from his home in Michigan in 1884 to inquire if Miss Mary Frye would take his eleven-year-old daughter Jessie "to board and teach her" in St. Andrews. He considered the local public school in Michigan too rough for little girls. The Beech Hill farm was about a mile and a half from the centre of St. Andrews, too far for a small girl to walk and in winter often much too snowy. Nell was likely first schooled at home by her cousin and de facto sister Ethel, who was seventeen and still at Beech Hill in 1881 when Nell reached six, the starting age at the free public school. By 1886, however, Ethel had met and become engaged to the Reverend W. Stanley Emery of Boston, who in late August of that year came to Beech Hill for the regulation inspection by Bella and George. The couple married in January 1887 and went to live in Wolfboro, New Hampshire. By this time, Nell, now eleven, was attending school in St. Andrews. "Nellie is at last I think beginning to warm up to her lessons," wrote her Aunt Helen to Susan Mowat in March 1888. "She is a dear child very affectionate, and quite talented...If she had only more perseverance and accuracy, she would do better. She has grown so much that I can hardly realize she is the wee 'Trot' that gave her new aunt such a loving welcome years ago."

In October 1888, George and Bella, obviously pleased with thirteen-year-old Nell, agreed that she should enjoy a taste of modest independence. At the end of October, she would visit, on her own, Ethel and Stanley in Wolfboro. Her adventure began with a voyage to Boston: first, by steamer from St. Andrews to Eastport, and then, by another steamer from Eastport to Portland and Boston. For the boat journey Nell was placed in the care of Professor J. Emery Hoar and Mrs. Hoar of Brookline, Massachusetts, who were returning home at the end of the summer season. The Hoars were among the first summer visitors to St. Andrews to buy property and establish their own summer house. They renovated and enlarged a house near Beech Hill to which they gave the name Risford (now Tara Manor Inn). George Mowat supervised the building work for Professor Hoar. On June 10, 1885, when sending George money to pay the builders "at your discretion" for work done so far, the professor asked him to "tell Nellie I am delighted that she takes an interest in Risford; how I would like to receive a written account of the place from her, illustrated by some of her graphic little pictures." This note was the first acknowledgement of her artistic gifts from someone outside the home. Her mother, Nell would often remark ironically years later, thought she was a "genius" because she liked to draw and paint from an early age.

The visit to Ethel in Wolfboro was perhaps the opening gambit in

Bella's long-range plan for her talented daughter. Nell spent a week in Boston with Stanley Emery's mother and sisters, and then Ethel and Stanley came to accompany her on the last part of the journey. In Wolfboro, she attended a local school and at thirteen, she would have been considered old enough to be a mother's helper. Ethel now had one young child and was expecting another. After two months, Nell wrote to her family at Beech Hill to say that she was not homesick and wanted to stay until April. As it turned out, no permission was necessary because soon after her request,

Helen Mowat, Nell's aunt.
Courtesy of the Charlotte County Archives

Nell lost her appetite, acquired a "pallid look,"and was, in fact, quite ill for the first months of 1889. When she finally felt well enough to travel, George and Bella Mowat went to Wolfboro and brought her back to Beech Hill. In late April, her mother could write, with evident relief to her sister-in-law Susan, "We are so glad to have Nellie so well and at home again."

Exposure to a wider world seems to have had the desired effect upon Nell for she now became a better student. Helen remarked in a letter to Susan the following August, "I expect to send Brydone to school [in St. Andrews] as soon as they open and I'm sure it will be very good for him, as I think it has been for Nellie." Nell and Brydone walked to school in town together and ate most of their noontime meals at the home of their father's sister, Aunt Bessie McMaster. Bessie McMaster and her husband Sidney were a generous and kindly couple who had married late and had no children of their own, but took a keen and practical interest in their nieces and nephews. At the same time, Helen began giving lessons to Nell and to her second cousin May Morris, who was also fourteen years old.

"Nellie has begun lessons and next week May Morris will begin to learn with me, so with my own, I shall have quite a 'Dame's School,' only I won't use the *cedar*," she reported to Susan. A large upstairs room at the back of the house, above the kitchen and connected to it by a little stairway, was used as a warm and convenient nursery and dining room by Helen and her small children. Probably it now also became a schoolroom. It isn't clear what subjects she taught the two older girls and it is possible that they were simply receiving extra tutoring in subjects they found difficult at school. Another possibility is that Nell, at least, was learning the Latin she would need for the last stage of her schooling. "Nellie has been pegging away at her Latin tonight, she is getting on so nicely at school and her last report is capital...her teacher says she is one of his brightest scholars," wrote Helen in November 1890.

In August 1891, Nell began attending the Charlotte County Grammar School. The school had been built in 1818 and offered a curriculum at the secondary school level, leaning toward the classics in literature and languages. Nell was growing up at a time when educating girls beyond the age of sixteen or eighteen was unusual. She was fortunate in having enlightened parents who recognized her abilities and who had the means to help her develop them. She would also have been encouraged by her Aunt Helen, who had probably attended university. Finally, at the grammar school, she encountered William Brodie, a sympathetic and scholarly headmaster. Many years later Nell acknowledged her debt to him in the dedication of her first published book, *Funny Fables of Fundy*: Brodie was her "teacher, oracle and friend." To his encouragement of Nell as a writer and observer, we owe the detailed written descriptions of her next adventure, which began in the autumn of her eighteenth year.

"A Come Out Young Woman"

It was very lonely that night in Halifax seeing you sail away
into the dark. Cabby waited for me at the head of the wharf
and drove me to the Queen Hotel where I put in a wretched
night and started the next morning for Moncton at 7 o'clock
in a thick fog...Now dear little girl always remember you
have your own name to make. Never say a vulgar word or
do a vulgar action and come home better than you left which
is the wish & prayer of your Aft. Father, Geo Mowat.
— Letter from George Mowat to Nell Mowat
(December 12, 1893)

If travel and new settings were part of Bella Mowat's grand plan for
her daughter, then the next venture, for a Charlotte County farm
family of limited means, was truly ambitious. George Mowat had a
cousin, Julia Parker Legh, a widow who lived in Richmond Hill, a
suburb of London in England. In Richmond there was a school of
art and music, and George, Bella, and Julia must have agreed that
Nell would benefit from instruction there as well as from a sojourn in
London. "Aunt" Julia extended an invitation and arrangements were
made for Nell to spend six months with her and her daughter May,
attending art school from early December 1893 until the end of May
1894. Accompanying Nell from St. Andrews was her second cousin
Lilian Morris, like Nell a first-cousin-once-removed to Julia Legh.
Lily was twenty-one to Nell's eighteen, a graduate of the Charlotte
County Grammar School and deemed old enough to fill the role of
chaperone or companion for the voyage. The two young women were
setting out on a much modified version of the "grand tour," a visit to
the fount of the mainly British culture in which they had been raised

and a substitute for the finishing school and debut, or "coming out," that was more usual for middle and upper-class girls at the time.

Their voyage across the Atlantic aboard the Furness Line steamship *Damara* began on the evening of November 11, 1893. Nell's father had brought the young women by train to Halifax. The ship sailed shortly after they boarded, swallowed by darkness and leaving George Mowat suffering the pangs of loneliness he charmingly confessed to in one of his rare letters to Nell a month later. Once at sea, Lily and Nell fell immediately and severely seasick and were only just recovering when their ship was engulfed by an enormous Atlantic storm that roared for three days. It was not until they had been on board a week that Nell was able to begin writing the weekly letters to her family that she sent whenever she was away from home during the next several years. This first letter was written in the chartroom of the *Damara*, to which the captain had made the passengers welcome, on Sunday, November 19, and it was written in pencil because the sea was still too rough to allow use of an open bottle of ink. It is the first example we have of Nell's literary ability (and often somewhat cavalier spelling and punctuation):

> Well of the first few days off Halifax I have but an indistinct and not very pleasant recollection! I have some idea that I was dragged out on deck by some one and deposited on a steamer chair with a shawl around my legs. I think some one must have dragged me back again too but I don't remember about that. But on Thursday a storm arose which raged all Friday and did not die down untill Saturday night...The steward said if we'd only seen the storms he'd seen we would not call this half a storm but it was bad enough for me. Don't you talk about waves until you see them in a storm on the Atlantic, when the light of day is obscured by a huge one rising before your port hole and then bursting with a bang like a cannon and sending the ship down on the other side untill the force of gravity hardly knows

whichway to act, and above the noise of the wind and
waves you can hear the sound of breaking glass and
china to say nothing of the confusion caused by all your
worldly goods and chatels performing a hornpipe on
the floor of your cabin...And through all this Lilly and
I lay flat on our backs like sculptured saints with our
hands clasped in front and our elbows braced against
the sides of the berth and our eye fixed on a couple of
life preservers suspended from the ceiling.

Once the storm had passed, and everyone recovered, they had "a
glorious time," playing cards till nearly eleven o'clock. "The captain,"
she noted "is great fun."

When the *Damara* came in sight of land again — the Scilly Isles
on November 23 — and entered the English Channel, Nell gave all
her attention to the new landscape that began scrolling along the port
side of the vessel. With the kindly captain acting as a tour guide, and
by summoning the geography she had learned from Mr. Brodie, she
absorbed as much as her hungry eyes and mind would permit. Like all
young English Canadians, she was as familiar with the landscape and
place names of England as she was with those of her own country.
Over and over, she was reminded of Mr. Brodie's English literature
and geography lessons. In one letter to her mother, after listing the
names of places and describing landforms, colours, and effects of light
and atmosphere, she noted quite simply, "We just stood and looked
with all our eyes."

Nell and Lily were met at the London docks on November 26 by
their young cousin May Legh, who took them by train to Richmond.
From the station it was a short walk to her mother's house, Rothesay
Cottage, at 18 King's Road, Richmond Hill, and they arrived in time
for five o'clock tea. The Leghs expressed general relief at their safe
passage because the Atlantic storm that battered the *Damara* had
wrecked many smaller vessels in the Channel. Promptly the next
morning May walked Nell and Lily to the Richmond School of Art
and Music on Halford Road so that Nell could enroll in drawing

classes. "I am to take regular lessons on Monday and Wednesday mornings. On Tuesdays I attend a course of lectures on perspective and I go on Fridays for practice," she wrote her mother. (Lily also enrolled at the school but whether in the graphic art or music section isn't known; neither her letters to her family nor the records of the Richmond School of Art and Music have survived.) At the school they were pleasantly surprised by the warmth of the English girls. Nell had been told that they were reserved until they knew you, but she found them to be very welcoming and, in general, "much nicer than I expected to find them."

The relaxed schedule left Nell and Lily, with May as guide, enough free time to explore Richmond and, in due course, the city and surrounding countryside. Richmond, Nell found, "a perfectly beautiful place. I never saw anything like the terrace gardens in all my life." Many of the houses were surrounded by holly hedges and the walls covered with ivy. "Oh Mrs. Peters," she wrote in one letter, "I think your England is a perfect heaven upon earth." Within a day or two of arriving, they walked in nearby Richmond Park where Nell was impressed by the deer feeding quietly and — like any colonial child of that period, raised on a steady diet of English literature — by the large oak trees: "The big oak trees are something grand, everything is like a picture or a story book." A visit to the Royal Botanic Gardens at Kew, which adjoins Richmond and lies within the same loop of the Thames River, soon followed. Although Nell remarked on the splendid display of exotica she saw at Kew — the palms, orchids, and huge chrysanthemums — and later mentioned the possibility of writing an article about the gardens for the St. Andrews newspaper, it was English wildflowers, gathered on many subsequent outings in the countryside, that most delighted her. Early on, she began a sketch book, and the following April, she wrote to her mother from Hemel Hempstead, where she and Lily were staying with friends or relatives of the Morris family: "Last Monday I spent the morning in painting some English daisies. I am going to try and do as many of the wild flowers as I can in my English book of sketches, I have done some primroses and gorse and several other little things." Her pleasure in

Halford House (home of the Richmond School of Art and Music),
circa 1868. 1920s issue of *The Listener*

flowers, dating from her childhood rambles in the woods and fields at
Beech Hill, was quickened by encounters with species she had known
only from books. She names cowslips; white, yellow, and purple cro-
cuses; wallflowers; squills; quantities of little yellow celandine; and
the mysterious blackthorn blossoms, which emerge in the spring,
before the leaves, as drifts of white on dense, grey hedgerows.
There are also many references, beginning soon after her arrival in
Richmond, to helping with flower arranging at the Leghs' church.
The Leghs were Anglicans and the entire household attended as many
as four services on a Sunday. (Nell also took partial responsibility for
a Sunday school class.) Reviewing the events of the previous six days,
she told her family on May 14: "Saturday we devoted to decorating the
church for Whit Sunday [the seventh after Easter] & it looks simply
perfect all white & red flowers...Everyone says the choir stalls look
lovely, we did them with white narcissus & double red geraniums &
hot house ferns."

When corresponding with her family Nell made an effort to write
about subjects that would interest not only her parents but also the
aunts, uncles, and cousins who would read her letters or hear them

read aloud. Reading aloud was a household custom. The letters contained evocative descriptions of people, customs, and places and were couched in terms acceptable to a mixed audience. They also featured occasional wry comments as, for example, when she applauded her parents for the "respectful way" in which they broached the subject of her defective grammar. Her letters to Beech Hill were often long and evidently written at top speed. Knowing how eagerly they were awaited, grammar, syntax, and punctuation were sacrificed to the need to get the the facts down on paper and into the mail as regularly as possible. Her meaning, however, was always clear and her one concession to the rules was the hasty aside: "have no time to read this over, know it is full of mistakes." The letters she wrote to people outside the immediate family, such as those to her contemporary and dearest girlhood friend, Alice Parker, another second cousin, were not saved. These must have taken an entirely different tone containing, one suspects, more pointed comments about people and the Richmond scene. While tidying her desk in St. Andrews a few years later, Alice wrote, "I have... been reading over the letters you wrote me from Richmond, I simply couldn't heave them, they were too funny..."

Relatives in England, and friends who had previous associations with St. Andrews, spared no effort in making a success of Lily's and Nell's six-month "season" in London. Prominent among them were the Osburns. Henry Osburn had been the St. Andrews manager of the New Brunswick and Canada Railway before retiring with his wife Eliza to the London suburb of Clapham in his native England. Before Nell left for London, he had offered to be her banker, providing cash whenever she needed it. Nell would let her father know the amount and George Mowat would then deposit an equivalent amount in Canadian currency to Henry Osburn's credit in the Bank of Nova Scotia in St. Andrews. Harry Moody, then deputy secretary but soon to be chief secretary of the Canadian Pacific Railway in London, and his wife Florence, yet another Mowat cousin, entertained them for lunch at their home in the London suburb of Carshalton soon after their arrival. Harry took the trouble to write reassuringly and immediately to Nell's father, "My dear George...I don't think Bella and you need be under any apprehension as to the effects the voyage had on [the two girls], as they both seem perfectly well and, Nelly especially, in highest spirits . . ." It was arranged that Aunt Julia, May, and Nell would spend Christmas Day with the Moodies, while Lily would go to her relatives the Amblers in Hemel Hempstead for a couple of weeks. Nell was invited to stay on at the Moodies for the remaining five days of Christmas week, after which she visited the Osburns in Clapham for the first week of the new year. There were easy train connections between Richmond, Clapham, and Carshalton, which allowed a good deal of social exchange among the three house-holds throughout this six-month period.

During another week-long stay in Clapham in May, the Osburns took Nell and Lily into the city to see Edward, Prince of Wales (1841-1910) and several other royals as they proceeded to the opening of the Royal Academy of Music. Two days later, the girls and the Osburns attended a royal "Drawing Room" at Buckingham Palace. The drawing-room ceremonies were formal assemblies at which young debutantes were presented to members of the royal family. That day it was the turn of Edward and Alexandra, Prince and Princess of Wales, to preside. Afterwards Henry Osburn pulled out all the stops by invit-ing Nell, Lily, and his wife and daughter to take tea at his club. This was followed by a visit to a French gallery to look at watercolours and then by a walk through the Burlington Arcade, which still today contains some of London's most exclusive shops. The very next evening the Osburns took them to see Gilbert and Sullivan's latest comic opera, *Utopia,* at the Savoy Theatre. This last treat Nell found "very good & very amusing" but, surprisingly for a person who later wrote plays and took part in amateur dramatic productions, she added, "I would not mind much if I thought I should never go inside a theatre again. I like the concerts in St. James Hall much better." Two orato-rios, one performed in St. Paul's Cathedral in January and one at St. Peter's Eton Square in March, by contrast, elicited superlatives.

On a later visit to St Paul's, which she would describe for readers of the *St. Andrews Beacon,* she admired the reredos and choir stalls carved by Grinling Gibbons, whose boyhood during the Great Plague she had read about in Austin Clare's *The Carved Cartoon*. Among the monuments, those of Wellington, Macauley, Nelson, and Sir Joshua Reynolds caught her eye, as well as, in the crypt, a recently installed bust of Sir John A. McDonald. Unaware of the installation, she and Lily both remarked that the "old chap" looked uncannily like Sir John A. From the crypt they climbed to the library and then up more steps to the whispering gallery where another old chap, but one still breathing, demonstrated the remarkable acoustics. More steps took them to the dome and a panoramic view of London. Another day they "did the city" at ground level, riding on the top of a bus from Trafalgar Square.

Most of Nell and Lily's sightseeing and cultural excursions were generally available to visitors to London — Kew Gardens, Westminster Abbey, St. Paul's Cathedral, and Hampton Court, to name a few — but some they owed to their association with Julia and May Legh and to the timing of their English visit. Luckily for Nell and Lily, the Leghs were cultivated women, disinclined to a retiring life despite their lack of male escorts. Queen Victoria might have thought that feminists "ought to get a good whipping," but royal disapproval failed to brake the momentum toward equal rights for women. A "ladies' college" education for daughters of the middle class no longer led automatically to marriage or dependent spinsterhood. Although they were not allowed to take degrees, some women were studying in the established universities or otherwise preparing for professional and semi-professional careers. Aunt Julia, even if she was not an active campaigner, seems to have been sympathetic with the general aims of the movement and did all that she could to encourage her daughter May, and Nell and Lily, to lead intellectually active and independent lives. As well as hosting the young Canadians on their six-month season in England, she gave them small gifts of money so they could travel to see the sights, and to Nell's delight, she was "very good about letting us go round by ourselves and never worries about us, which is a great comfort."

The Leghs were committed churchwomen, and one of May's

"good works" took the unusual form of amateur dramatic entertainments performed for the residents of London's poorhouses or, in English parlance, workhouses. Only two weeks after they arrived in Richmond, Nell and Lily accompanied May and her troupe of four other actors to perform at the workhouse in Hammersmith, a neighbouring westerly suburb of London. They travelled there and back by train and bus on a dark, rainy December evening. Nell would have been familiar with the idea of a workhouse because there was a poorhouse in St. Andrews until the 1890s, but she could hardly have been prepared for the size and grimness of the stone buildings she entered that night. Here is part of her description of the Dickensian scene: "The Hammersmith Mission is a great big house, or rather a succession of houses, built around a quadrangle...the porter led us through the most outlandish places, we had to march across the quadrangle with all the paupers who were going to their tea, we had to wait in the passageway to the dining hall and the paupers all trooped past us, there were about 400 of them, I thought that the procession would never stop...the women all dressed alike."

Aunt Julia also made sure that they went to see the paintings at the Royal Academy show in the spring, and, throughout the winter, ensured that they regularly attended Monday evening lectures at the Richmond Athenaeum. These lectures aimed to enlighten a general audience took on diverse subjects: the Moors in Spain, the physics of colour, and British Imperial Federation were the subjects of three lectures Nell mentions having attended with the Leghs. But most interesting by far to a Canadian was a lecture illustrated with limelight images (electric lighting was not yet common), probably sponsored by the Canadian Pacific Railway. Nell described it in a letter to her family: "It was on Canada & the great North West, and of course we were deeply interested in it, it was given free with a view to emigration. The young man who lectures [has] been all over Canada and had lived out on several farms out West so that he might be able to judge better of farm life in Canada. He seems deeply interested in his subject. His voice had got quite Canadianized during the process and he spoke of his trunk instead of his 'box.' He also impressed upon

Halford House today. Courtesy of Diana Rees

the audience that houses in Canada were mostly built of wood and the audience all thought it very funny." From the lecture on British Imperial Federation, Nell learned that Canada, the centre of her world, was to the English still a remote frontier society: "It was awfully funny hearing Canada classed with Australia and the possessions in South Africa & other outlandish places."

Another unusual experience the Leghs arranged was a walking tour of London by a well-known author and notable authority on the history of the city. Walter Besant (1836-1901) was a novelist, historian, biographer, and critic, whose book *London*, had just been published and who was also president for many years of the Society of Authors. He would be knighted in 1895, the year following the one in which he conducted three young women on an exclusive tour. There is nothing to tell us how the Leghs had made his acqaintance, but he might well have been one of the lecturers invited to the Richmond Athenaeum. "He is a very nice unimposing looking little man with a long iron gray beard...not at all appalling," Nell wrote. "His conversation is most interesting as you may imagine for he knows london very well and has a history to tell of every place we passed." Mr. Besant led the small party mainly around Holborn, an interesting district of London not on most travellers' lists of sights but one containing the Smithfield Markets and the twelfth-century Church of St. Bartholomew and its associated priory and hospital. (The St. Bartholomew Hospital, also known as St. Barts, is the oldest in London.) Nearby is Charterhouse, founded as an ancient monastery but known mostly for its later use as a boys' school (attended by such famous men as Steele, Addison, and Thackeray). The young women must have been pleasingly lively and attentive because Besant was unstinting in his chivalry toward them. Nell reported: "He treated us to tea, gave us each a photograph of a little church he took us to see [St. Bartholemew's] & also got us each a little book about it. He got us our tickets home & would not let May pay him back. And this morning May got a letter from him to say that he was going to send us each a copy of his new book on London…I hope that when I get home you will all treat me with due respect."

But not all of Nell and Lily's excursions were high-minded exercises in pursuit of culture or the performance of good works. Only four days after they landed, Aunt Julia took Nell to Regent Street, in the very heart of London — a mecca for shoppers the world over. Nell needed a jacket or coat suitable for an English as opposed to a New Brunswick winter. They found one that pleased Nell very much and her enthusiastic description and sketch of it in a letter to her mother on December 3 is the first indication we have of her interest in style in clothing: "a beauty and very cheap too, only a guinea and a half…they had just been reduced…It is black with a large otter collar & otter down the front. (Otter is very much worn here this year.)…Regent Street is a fine place, everyone looks as if they had just stepped out of the *Ladies Pictorial.*" Back home in Beech Hill, a dressmaker had been at the farm for the past two days making a winter coat for Nell's mother. Bella described her coat to Nell in a letter written on December 10: "It is made of serge and trimmed with some of my old Astrakhan coat…I was sorry to have to go to the expense of getting anything new for myself but I could not go to Church for three Sundays as I had nothing warm enough to wear. Have you tried to get a coat for yourself and how much will it cost? We will try and send you some money as soon as we can but father has not been able to sell any of his crop yet. We hope times may be better after a while." In that same letter, Bella told Nell she had collected twenty eggs from her flock that day and hoped soon to be getting four or five dozen a day: "they are a very good price now."

This exchange between a girl taking her first semi-independent steps and a self-denying mother, who does not dissemble about where the money comes from, is timeless. That Nell was fully aware of the cost of her stay in England is demonstrated repeatedly in her letters. She never forgot the price of eggs. When, in mid-April, Bella's hens were laying thirty eggs a day, Nell wrote, "I am glad your hens are doing so well you could make quite a lot if you could only send them over here, fresh eggs are selling in Richmond for [one and a half pence] each that is 36 cents per doz."

Four months later, the otter-trimmed jacket was too warm for spring wear and Nell considered buying a cape to replace it. She and her mother discussed the matter by mail. Bella gave her approval but cautioned Nell that although capes were very pretty, they were not becoming to everyone. She was more concerned with the state of Nell's dresses, boots and shoes, urging her not to "go *shabby*." Nell, however, had the bit between her teeth and reported : "I got a simply lovely new cape the other day and it was only 18s9p, that was very little for such a good one. I hope you don't think it was too much to pay for a cape for this will be a very useful one, nice & long & a very good color, kind of a grayish-brown, won't show the dust... and will last me for a long time. I have still an unbroken sovereign and will keep it in case of necessity... Concerning boots and shoes, I do not admire the English style of these... & I do not think I will have to invest in any until I come home, I hope not." By converting the prices of her jacket and cape into 1894 Canadian dollars — the otter-collared jacket would have cost $4.68 and the cape, $4.50 — and comparing these to the prices Bella Mowat was getting for a dozen eggs at the time — 14c in St. Andrews or 20c in St. Stephen — it's clear that Nell had not been a spendthrift. She was obviously pleased to be able to write: "My cape is most becoming, everyone says it looks so nice...I don't think my clothes are very shabby but I will try to get a new spring dress...You have been so good about sending me money but I don't want to be too extravagant for fear I will be short just before I leave & I will have a good many expenses then." What mother could require better evidence of a young daughter's appreciation and good sense?

Exposure to English life and culture was an important part of Nell's London education, but the main item on her daily curriculum was the drawing instruction she received at the Richmond School of Art and Music. Her reports about her lessons are usually brief and provide only a rough outline of the course of study. The first such report was in early December: "I have begun work at the art school and like it very much, although, of course, I only take the elementary until Xmas...I like Mr. Webb, my teacher at the art school, very much, he is quite elderly and very precise." In January she was "working in charcoal" and then there was no report of drawing lessons for many weeks, causing her mother to remark in mid-March, "You do not mention your drawing lessons but I was glad to know through Lilian that you are getting on nicely with them." This mild rebuke prompted a duly contrite reply: "I am sorry that I neglected to mention my drawing lessons...I *suppose* I got mixed up [she had written of them to someone else]. I am getting on pretty well I think...doing the life model in chalk...I shall ask Mr. Webb to give an opinion on the subject." Studies of a life model took up the next few weeks and proved satisfying to Nell and satisfactory to her instructor: "We have a fine model sitting...I am doing her very nicely if you want my opinion on the subject. Mr. Webb says it is getting on very well if you want his." Her family could also judge her progress from the sketches (for example, of the otter-collared jacket and the Hampton Court maze) that illustrated her letters. At Christmas, she also sent them a hand-painted card that would have one of the earliest examples in the series of original Christmas cards Nell sent to family and friends over the years.

Nell had promised Mr. Brodie that she would write her former fellow students at the Charlotte County Grammar School about her experiences in England. By February she had seen enough sights to be able to write what she called a "lengthy epistle" to them, remarking in a letter to her mother, "I don't think there was anything very interesting in it." Her own diffidence about the quality of her letter was not shared by Mr. Brodie and his students, nor by the enterprising editor of the *St. Andrews Beacon*. As soon as he read the letter, Robert Armstrong sought permission to publish an excerpt in his newspaper, where it appeared on March 1, 1894. Although it was not intended for print, "London Through Young Eyes" was Nell's first published writing. Skillfully composed and pitched to her school friends at home, the article built on details and themes they would have studied together, and included an anecdote about Lord Kilmarnock, or William Boyd, the fourth Earl of Kilmarnock (1704-1746). Relatively few visitors to the Tower of London would have been aware that this Scottish laird, who was beheaded on Tower Hill in 1746 for his part in the Jacobite uprising of 1745, had a connection to North America. But Nell, the proud great-granddaughter of Loyalists, was steeped in the lore of St. Andrews and had heard the then current explanation for the name of Kilmarnock Head on the northwest shore of Passamaquoddy Bay. (It is now thought that the name of the headland was more likely bestowed by James Boyd, probably a member of a collateral branch of the Boyd family, which was centred in the town of Kilmarnock in Scotland. James Boyd was in the Passamaquoddy region from 1763 to 1778 and held land grants and reserves from the Nova Scotia government on large tracts in the area.)

Lily Morris's father had redirected his subscription to the *Beacon* to Richmond Hill for the duration of the girls' visit, so Nell was able to see her letter in print. She thought it "great fun" and found the headings "perfectly killing." After thinking about it for a week, she added, "Had I known when I wrote it that it was destined to appear in print then there are one or two things I would have altered, however it does not matter." Her mother reported favourable local comment on the article and the editor must have indicated he would be glad to

Christmas card by Nell of Beech Hill farm. Courtesy of Ross Memorial Museum

have more because she encouraged Nell and Lily to write something together. But their remaining time in England was fast running out in a flurry of social engagements, sightseeing, and work at the art school. Nell allowed archly that she might be inspired to do some writing "for the press" after she returned home and had more time.

By mid-April, Nell and Lily were corresponding with the Furness Line agent to book their passage home to Canada and learned that its steamer *Halifax City* was due to sail at the end of May. Aunt Julia encouraged them to stay on into June if there was a suitable vessel, and Nell herself rather hoped the latter would be the case. She was thoroughly enjoying herself in England and wrote to her family, "I will be sorry to say goodbye to Richmond for we have so many interests there and have made so many friends that it will be almost like leaving home and it is not likely we will ever see it again." Her sojourn in the rich-textured London scene had worked: her young sensibilities were being attuned to subjects as disparate as architecture and social rituals. She acknowledged that she had "no idea what an interesting study architecture was" and as for English customs, commented, "English people think it awfully low to answer the door. I'm sure I don't know why, I think it's rather fun." George and Bella had another wish for Nell, less important to her intellectual development but symbolically important to them. No daughter of a long line of Loyalists should spend six months in London without seeing Queen Victoria. So Nell was happy to report, after a mid-May tour of Windsor Castle, "tell Dad I have at last seen the Queen. She was driving in the grounds with the Princess Louise."

As the date for their return approached, Bella Mowat began to think ahead and expressed concern about how Nell would adjust to life in St. Andrews after the excitements of England. Nell replied reassuringly with, as it turned out, unfounded optimism: "I am sure I will be quite ready to go to work again [helping her mother] when I go home and will not find St. Andrews at all dull." The sailing date of the *Halifax City* was a little delayed, until June 10, so Nell got her wish for a few more days in England, and she let her parents know to expect her home again after the twentieth of the month. With her newly acquired sense of independence, she asked them not to make any arrangements for the journey from Halifax to Saint John — she and Lily would make their own way. Nell was coming home "better" than she left, as enjoined by her father, although he no doubt had her moral character, not her self-confidence, in mind. But the latter was the natural result of her wider exposure to experience. She was ready to take on responsibility: "I am glad to hear you are not planning to chaperone me when I get back for I suppose I may then be considered the 'come out young lady' you were always talking about."

A Practical Schooling in Art

In spite of Nell's reassurances to her mother, the return to St. Andrews proved more difficult than she had anticipated. No lively nineteen-year-old coming back to a small, remote town in Canada after six exhilarating months in a large European city, far less one as engrossing as London, could hope for an untroubled re-entry. Nell's first cousin Owen Campbell, a young banker in Saint John eight years her senior, became a sympathetic confidant. Owen had arranged to meet Nell's ship in Saint John and had the arrangement not broken down, he might have been able to warn her of the difficulties ahead. Five months after her return, in November 1894, he replied to what must have been a doleful letter from Nell: "I was very glad to find you still in existence but very sorry to hear of your having the blues. Reasoning may be a very good method of getting rid of them but it seems to me you need a change of some sort or other...I see you are going through the same stage of disgust with the world in general that I did and having no congenial people to talk to about it, your position is a sort of 'pleasing God, *enduring* him forever and not wanting to — *or seeing why you should.*'"

On the failure of her family to appreciate her unease, a subject which must have figured prominently in Nell's letter, Owen offered this observation: "They...have nothing but *experience* of a sort, which they persistently push down your throat when afflicted by any disease mental or physical, how can you expect any appreciation on their part of the troubles to which human nature is subject at a certain stage of existence which I fancy not all by any means bother their heads about." He returned to the theme in a long letter, written almost a year later:

> You mention and *more* than mention the fact that the elders of your household (by which I don't mean Uncle George, although he is one in the strictest sense of the word) take the very greatest interest in the books you read not in the proper sense of the word but very much in the spirit of the Inquisitors of old or the Pope himself, who is said to be such an excellent judge of literature of every description that he decides just what the faithful *shall* or *shall not* inwardly digest. Now, of course, you anticipate that I shall thoroughly sympathize with you in your struggle for freedom if you like to give it as grand a name but at the same time, I would suggest that your present course seems to me the very wisest you can pursue under the circumstances. Always remember that the older members of the human family have what they consider their rights, that people with conservative instincts are never afraid of the old house toppling about their ears but as the little boys say "do hate like blazes" to see anything new going up, not because they have the ghost of a chance of inhabiting the place but because they think it absolutely unsafe for you.

Nell's "present course" appears to have been less a matter of paddling her way out of troubled waters than of keeping afloat — of coming to terms with life at Beech Hill and settling into the busy, if not always satisfying, cultural life of the town. There is little documentary evidence to go on. During this period, Nell wrote and received relatively few letters. In December 1894, her married cousin Ethel

Emery commented: "What an energetic body you are with your clubs and societies," adding that if their lives were compared, she would be perceived the country mouse and Nell the town or the city one. On February 27, 1896, the *St. Andrews Beacon* reported that "Miss Nellie Mowatt read a paper on the purpose of Tennyson's 'In Memoriam' to the Greenock Church Literary Society." W. J. Richardson considered the form and structure of the poem and Nell the meaning and purpose. At home she helped

Owen Campbell, Nell's cousin.
Courtesy of the Charlotte County Archives

around the house and the dairy, sketched and painted, and when in need of a change, spent time with relatives. In May 1895, for example, she stayed for several weeks with her uncle John Campbell and his wife in Moncton.

This frustrating, or at least desultory, interlude in Nell's life lasted for almost two-and-a-half years. In the fall of 1896, or possibly January 1897, she enrolled in the Woman's Art School of the Cooper Union in New York City. Nell, now twenty-two, evidently had decided that her future lay with painting and drawing, and in applied or commercial rather than fine art.

Founded in 1859, the Cooper Union was the legacy of Peter Cooper, a wealthy, self-made American inventor and manufacturer whose aim was to equip young men and women of modest means for life in a commercial and industrial society. Instruction at the Cooper Union was in science, art, and technology, and for those admitted, tuition was free. All applications required the signature of a guarantor who would vouch for the applicant's inability to pay for instruction. For Nell and her parents, free tuition was an obvious attraction. The other attraction was the presence of her cousin Ethel Emery who had recently moved from Wolfboro, New Hampshire, to New York with her minister husband Stanley and their three young children.

In the late 1890s, the Woman's Art School of the Cooper Union received twice as many applications as there were places. In 1897, 509 women applied and 265 were admitted. After two months, this number had shrunk to 236 "by the natural sifting of incompetence, mistaken vocation and like disabilities." Mary A. Vinton, the school's fair but firm principal, did not mince words in her annual reports. Of the 236 who survived the first few months, only 197 made it through to the end of the year. The next year told a similar story: 293 admissions from 401 applicants were reduced after three months to 240. Competition made for a demanding regime; "dead wood" was quickly eliminated. The students, all between the ages of sixteen and thirty-five, were allowed a three-month trial period in each class to demonstrate competence, and those who failed to do so were required to leave. In her annual report for 1900, Mary Vinton stated that the school's exacting standards had taught the community "that it is wiser to place their daughters at once in the way of other callings than to waste their time in experiment." She was determined, as was her predecessor Susan M. Carter, that the Woman's Art School should not be regarded as a finishing school where young women might while away a few years between high school and marriage. "In earnest, serious attention to work," she wrote in her 1897 report, "and in the observance of orderly conduct, the record of the school has never been better." Mary Vinton might not have been a feminist in the modern sense but she believed that all women should be able to earn a living.

The quid pro quo for free tuition was that successful applicants had to support themselves. Students were encouraged to find part-time or occasional employment in fields related to their studies. In 1898, combined student earnings in design and illustration, miniature painting, and teaching amounted to $7,000. The school's objective was to turn out highly employable students who would work in offices, workshops, and classrooms, not languish in garrets. For the diploma students in art, the two main avenues of employment were education, chiefly in the public schools, and — in an age when the prototypes for posters, advertisements, printed illustrations, and catalogues had to be hand drawn or painted — illustration and design. For prospective teachers, the school provided technical training in working with clay and wood, as well as instruction in painting and drawing. The latter were approached as crafts in the workaday medieval sense, rather than as fine art. The painter as "artist," as distinct from craftsman or craftswoman, was a Renaissance conception. Mary Vinton, a medievalist in this sense, made no bones about the school's orientation in her 1890 annual report: "In any educational institution the genius — the brilliant student — is the exception; it is the benefit accruing to the large average of its students by which its value is reckoned; and so in this institution of art, while a comparatively small number may make a name in the world as artists, a large proportion, either wholly or in part, make a living."

For the future founder of Cottage Craft, the Cooper Union's philosophy could hardly have been more appropriate and Nell thoroughly absorbed its lessons. In her annual reports, Mary Vinton emphasized repeatedly the importance of application and intelligence as distinct from mere talent: "It is not always the most talented who make the best record in the race for self-support. Tact; persistent enterprise in searching for work; intelligent study of the changing requirements of manufacturers — in short, business qualities, are the most potent factors in success." The school's alumnae helped bolster its business orientation. In 1900, the Alumnae and Students Association of the Woman's Art School, with support from the Society of Associated Designers (founded by three graduates of the school), inaugurated a class in pen and ink illustration to serve the market for designers and illustrators and to keep students abreast of current trends and styles. The Alumnae Association also took care of the inner woman. In 1897, it set up a lunchroom to provide students with simple warm

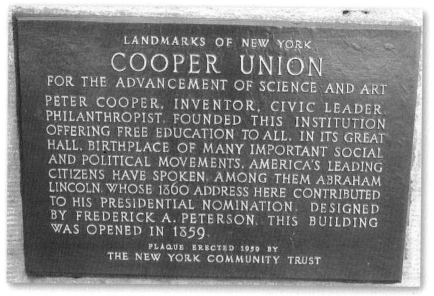

Wall plaque at the Cooper Union. Courtesy of Greg Cohane

food at cost (cold lunches being thought to be detrimental to the health of students), and in 1888/89 it went a step farther, handing out sixty lunch tickets monthly.

The Cooper Union, which flourishes still, is located in the East Village, two blocks east of Broadway in the so-called student quarter of Lower Manhattan. Immediately west of Broadway, in the same district, are New York University, Washington Square, and Greenwich Village. Nell lived at two addresses: 308 Second Avenue at East Seventeenth Street, during her first two years in the city, and west of Second Avenue at 214 East Twentieth Street during her third year. Both houses accommodated female students and were within six blocks of the Cooper Union. When Nell and her roommate, Augusta Graves, left for summer school in June 1898, they congratulated themselves on seeing the last of 308 Second Avenue, but the house was upscale enough to offer a manservant ("our man in buttons"). Male visitors were allowed but not, in the 1890s, in the rooms. At 308 Second Avenue, a Miss Clingsberg and her young man, who, Nell quipped, had been engaged for about 150 years, met in the parlour. The young man was the unofficial postman for the other residents.

Letters were placed on the hall table during his visits, and to signal that they were to be posted, the girls, not to disturb the courting couple, scratched on the parlour door. As well as being fairly Spartan, the rooms were not particularly well heated. In December 1897, Nell wrote Bella that some of the girls were reduced to "pinching" coal for their stove, as George the domestic wouldn't give them any extra. But at other times the rooms were comfortable enough for Nell, Augusta, and their friend "Texas," all students at Cooper, to read together the life of Jean-François Millet, champion of the French peasant and manual labour. According to Nell's letters, they talked of nothing but art and literature.

Outside her rooming house, Nell had two refuges: the Emerys' house on East Twenty-Eighth Street, which she visited regularly, and Grace Church and its associated Art Students Club. Nell, Augusta (always referred to as "Miss Graves" in Nell's letters), and "Texas" (whose given name was never revealed) were all denizens of the club. Established in 1896, the Art Students Club was the gift of Catharine Lorillard Wolfe, an extremely rich heiress who, among many other bequests, willed funds to Grace Church to be used for some form of "women's work." (Her largest bequest was to the Metropolitan Museum of Art; she was the only woman among the museum's 106 founders.) The funds left to Grace Church were used by the rector, Dr. Huntington, and Mrs. Newell, the widow of a former rector of the Episcopalian Church in Paris, to provide a sanctuary and meeting place for out-of-town women art students. They located it on the second floor of Grace House, built by the parish in 1881, between the church and the rectory. Mrs. Newell had established a similar club for young American art students in Paris. Although the New York club was under the wing of Grace Church, there was no requirement that students using it be members of the congregation. For students like Nell and her friends, the club offered pleasant, comfortable common rooms; an excellent library of books, magazines, and newspapers; and walls on which to hang paintings and sketches. It was open every day from ten in the morning to ten at night, with tea served every afternoon at four. Mary Vinton described it as "a blessing for students living in the typical boarding house." Mrs. Newell also helped particularly needy students, and in addition to tea, she was soon providing Sunday night suppers. These meals were a huge success and always crowded. Nell, one assumes, was a regular diner.

A third refuge in New York, metaphorical rather than actual, was Nell's correspondence with her mother and with her steadfast friend Mary Gove. Nell and Bella wrote weekly, and Mary frequently, so Nell was well informed about affairs at home. Thanks to a rail link and strong commercial and social connections between southern New Brunswick and the eastern seaboard of the United States, letters between St. Andrews and New York were delivered within — by current standards — an astonishing two days. A letter mailed in New York on Thursday would get to St. Andrews on Saturday. Mary was the daughter of Dr. Harry Gove, who practised medicine in St. Andrews. Five years younger than Nell, she was a lively and talented correspondent who conveyed the recent gossip, including her own romantic attachments, with tolerance and wit. She joked that when Nell eventually returned to St. Andrews she would have developed into "a regular bachelor girl with a cut away coat, stiff collar, etc., you know the sort of person I mean."

Although Nell's circumstances in New York were never straitened, she noted in a letter to her mother in March 1898 that, Lent notwithstanding, she accepted the offer "of a good square meal these days whenever I can get it." And a year later, in March 1899, she again commented on her shortage of cash: "I am awful economical these days and as Texas says, 'Nichols [*sic*] are getting to look as big as dinner plates and quarters like cart wheels.'" Nell used money or "tin" from home only to pay for essentials, depending for her other needs on what she could earn, and on what she described as "presents." These gifts usually took the form of invitations to dinner and tickets to exhibitions and theatre and opera matinees. "I work so hard at the School," she commented to her mother, "that I don't get much time to look around [for work]." In 1899, when living at East Twentieth Street, she and Augusta lightened their household expenses by taking a "boarder," for whom they provided dinner at 25c a meal. The boarder, who lived in the room below, was the cousin of a friend of Augusta's who had come to New York to cultivate her voice. Nell and Augusta found they could cook for three as cheaply as for two. Nell also made a little money by selling handmade Easter cards to members of Grace Church for 30c apiece and by accepting small commissions. In March 1898, she obtained an order for painting Easter boxes from a "swell stationers" on Fifth Avenue. The commission didn't pay particularly well, but Nell suggested in a letter home that it would help cover the expenses for a summer school later that year.

In addition to the daily classes at the Cooper Union, Nell attended, on average, three lectures a week at galleries, museums, the Art Students Club (associated with Grace Church), and the Art Students League. The latter, founded in 1875 by artists and students, many of them women, offered courses and studio space — but no degrees or diplomas — to those with a serious interest in the arts. "I am learning so much these days," Nell wrote to her mother in January 1899, "I sometimes fear my brain will crack." By March her brain was still intact, but Nell wondered how much more it could absorb: "I hope my brain won't give out. I went to two [lectures] last Sat." In spite of, or probably because of, a very busy schedule, Nell blossomed at Cooper and wrote no more glum letters to her cousin Owen. She felt the exhilaration that studying with gifted and demanding teachers could bring:

Mr. Twachtman walked through our alcove last Monday. And I came to the conclusion that I never knew before what inspiration meant. But it's a fact that the presence of that man brought back memories of the days when I used to be told that my work was atmospheric and sympathetic and so inspired me that after his departure I siezed a piece of charcoal and worked like desperation, for I felt my old spirit returning to me again. The result was so astonishing that Mr. Metcalf when he saw it the following day nearly fell off his chair. His surprise was so great that he forgot to

criticise it and only remarked: "Why that is so
much better than you have been doing."

In his own paintings, John Henry Twachtman was less concerned with
representing the appearance of objects and places than with expressing the feelings they evoked. He was also known — and this was an
example that Nell would eventually follow in New Brunswick — for
preferring quiet everyday landscapes to the dramatic or the spectacu-
lar. From Howard Chandler Christy, on the other hand, the instructor
in pen and ink illustration, as well as a supplementary sketch class
sponsored by the Alumnae Association, she learned that good art
requires more than fine feeling. It also requires vigour: "You can't do
a good drawing unless you put your whole strength into it and you
can't put your whole strength into it unless you have it to put, therefore, he argues that it is as much a part of your education to acquire
strength as anything else." Of Nell's instructors at the Cooper Union,
all of whom were accomplished, Christy would become the most
famous. In 1898, he covered the Spanish-American War in Cuba for
a number of magazines and during World War I, he drew posters for
the navy and the Red Cross. His "The Soldier's Dream" (later dubbed
"The Christy Girl") was an early pin-up. Christy was also a profuse
illustrator of books and a regular contributor to leading magazines,
including *Scribner's*, *Harper's*, *Century*, and *Ladies Home Journal*.

At Cooper, Nell was known as a serious student who adored Mary
Vinton and admired her instructors, but she was no humble acolyte.
Wanting to draw Moses Ebenezer, a Black man who was posing for
a portrait class in which she was not enrolled, Nell sat in the room
one morning as if she belonged and made the sketch. Miss Vinton
came in, saw Nell, but did not chide her. Had she done so Nell would
have told her that Moses Ebenezer was "so lovely" that she wanted
a sketch of him as a gift for her father. In the same letter to her
mother, Nell admitted that she had received a "blowing up" from
Mr. Metcalf, her least favourite instructor, and had tried but failed to
"feel penitential." It was an Ash Wednesday, she reasoned, and in "a
free country the people don't curse their enemies on Ash Wednesday."

The Cooper Union in New York City today. Courtesy of Greg Cohane

Willard L. Metcalf, a well-known landscape painter and illustrator, was the teacher of Nell's morning class in life and cast drawing (drawings made from the plaster casts of celebrated sculptures). A month later, in March 1898, she wrote: "I…gave Mr Metcalf a blowing up last week and next time he came round he was very decent."

To enable students to sketch and keep in touch with their craft during the long vacation, the active and influential Alumnae Association introduced an outdoor sketch class in the spring of 1898. Nell spent at least one day sketching on Staten Island in a class conducted by Hugo Froelich. For Nell and some of the other students, this outing was a prelude to a summer school at Lakeview, near Stroudsburg, Pennsylvania. Miss Vinton was keen that she should attend, as was fellow student Edith Levin at whose parents' house she would stay. Miss Levin, Nell commented cryptically to her mother, wanted so much to get "all the blue blood into the class she can" that she required no immediate commitment from Nell. There are no details of the syllabus, but Nell expected to be out of doors all of the time.

The work, as she explained to her mother, would be very different from the cast work at Cooper.

At Stroudsburg in early June, Nell, Augusta, and Miss Levin, who had travelled together by train from New York, were met by an old man who took them and their trunks in a "carry all affair." The old man Nell described as "the greatest sketch." He used to be a "preacher of the word" until he abandoned his calling, in order, as he put it, to carry "strangers" around the country. The road was hilly and took them through beautiful woods where all kinds of lovely wildflowers grew. The Levins' house was on a high ridge twelve hundred feet above sea level in the Kittanning Hills. The verandah at the front of the house, "covered with climbing roses that reach ... up to the roof," looked onto a valley with a small lake. In exchange for their room and board, Nell and Augusta had agreed to wash up after meals, polish the glasses and silver, tidy and dust the drawing-room, and wait at table. To make the terms as reasonable as possible for the other girls, Mrs. Levin did all the cooking herself and engaged only one servant — to do the rough work. Nell and Augusta had also agreed to do some sewing, as the Levins' house needed curtains. Tuition was one or two dollars per week, and for this Nell needed help from home. In a March letter to her mother, she intimated that she hoped to earn enough in New York to see her through June, but after June, she would probably have to be subsidized.

At the Levins' house, Nell also came to know Edith's father, an unkempt but courteous and cultivated man of eccentric or, as Nell thought her mother might have said, "peculiar" habits and ideas. Mr. Levin stayed at the house year-round and did a little farming in a very small way. Miss Vinton thought highly of him. Nell was intrigued by his library, finding on the same shelf a wonderfully eclectic collection that included Thomas Henry Huxley, Herbert Spencer, the Koran, the Bible, and the Book of Common Prayer. During a walk together through his fields and vineyards, Mr. Levin was delighted that Nell was able to identify some of the flowers that he could not name.

The regime at the beginning of the summer was far from rigorous: "a little sewing and writing and a sketch occasionally." There were so many wild strawberries, blackberries, huckleberries, and wild grapes in the neighbourhood that she and Augusta considered buying sugar and preserving some fruit for their housekeeping in the coming year. During rest periods on the verandah, Nell, Augusta, and Edith read aloud George Eliot's *Felix Holt*. Nell also would have liked to play golf and tennis — at Lakeview there was a golf links, or at least a few holes, and a tennis court was being laid out — but she had not brought her clubs, balls, or racquet. By the 1890s, golf and tennis were popular games in St. Andrews and were among the few that women could play without, as was thought then, loss of decorum.

With the arrival of the instructors, William L. Lathrop and John Henry Twachtman, in early July, things began to "spin." The house filled with students from the Cooper Union and Philadelphia, and classes were organized. Nell wrote of "heaping up knowledge wholesale." Lathrop, a teacher of *plein air* or outdoor landscape painting — whose interest in the students was "such a contrast to Mr. Metcalf"— exceeded her "wildest expectations." He and "our beloved Mr. Twachtman," Nell wrote to her mother, were close friends who had once roomed together. Like Nell herself, Lathrop was "ris" on a farm and claimed to have found his calling while sitting behind a plow. But "Eddie" (possibly a nickname for Mr. Twachtman) dismissed this as an affectation, an idea acquired only after he came to New York. Lathrop taught them an entirely new method of using watercolour, making them work a long time — three mornings in one case — upon a single sketch.

In the spring of 1898, Nell, for the first time in her weekly letters to her mother, raised the subject of her future. She was, she wrote, "much concerned" about it. Miss Vinton thought that she might be appointed as a pupil teacher if she came back the following year. The position would carry a small honorarium, but Nell's constant need for money turned her thoughts to permanent paid employment. Her first choice was to work as an illustrator but the conventional wisdom at Cooper was that it was almost impossible to do good illustrating without taking the life class. The alternative was to look for a position immediately in, as she put it: "some boarding school round home

where they don't know much about art and would think two years
studying in New York and a diploma from Cooper all that is required.
You might ask aunt Helen if she thinks I would have any show in the
Rothesay School. Perhaps I could get a position there if I taught art
and something else though what the Dickens something else could be
I don't know. I should prefer Windsor [King's College in Nova Scotia]
but expect they know too much there."

Aunt Helen may not have been encouraging, and it is unlikely that
Nell, whose heart was not set on teaching, approached the Rothesay
School or King's College. She returned to Cooper for the life class
in the fall of 1899, but not as a pupil teacher, and graduated with
a diploma the following May. She received first-grade certificates in
Elementary Cast Drawing (1897), Drawing from the Antique (1898),
and Drawing from Life (1899). Augusta Graves was the silver medal-
list in the Drawing from the Antique class. In addition to the classes
required for her diploma, Nell had attended a class in illustration.
At the end of the 1898 school year, she told her mother that "working in the illustration" had so distracted her that she was afraid that
she would not get her first-grade certificate in the Antique. Nell also
attended lectures in anatomy by Thomas Eakins of *The Rower* fame
and lectures in perspective by Frederick Deilman. Through the heavy
schedule of lectures and exhibitions, Nell emerged from New York
with a solid grounding in European and American art. Among the
few lectures mentioned in her letters home — Bella Mowat and Mary
Gove had little interest in the history of art — were ones on the
arts and crafts of the Middle Ages and the paintings of Jean-François
Millet. She also referred to a "most wonderful exhibition of Japanese
fabrics, the first I have ever seen," at the American Art Galleries: "We
nearly went crazy over them in fact I never thought Japanese things
could be so beautiful."

In the winter and spring of 1899, with her days at the Cooper
Union definitely coming to an end, Nell began to look in earnest for
jobs. In January, she asked her mother to send a copy of the *Canadian
Churchman* so that she could apply for positions in church schools.
The chief attraction of teaching, after several years of being short of

Sketches by Nell done at the Cooper Union, 1897.

Courtesy of Anthony E. Hilditch

"tin," was the prospect of a guaranteed salary. In February, she also wrote to her friend Alice Parker, now in Toronto, to ask about teaching opportunities there. Alice, who was taking a class in watercolour, was not very optimistic. Competition was keen, and in Toronto there were so many well-known artists who taught (among them several who would become members of the Group of Seven). However, Alice promised to make inquiries and to let Nell know if anything turned up. In mid-March, Nell wrote her mother to tell her that she had almost abandoned the idea of getting a school, and that she would be better off to take a position in some large illustrating house where she could learn some of the techniques of reproduction. The salary would be small but she would learn much more than she would at teaching. She mentioned that she had a few places in mind and anticipated no difficulty in finding the work she wanted.

However, May of 1899 saw Nell not knocking on the doors of

illustrating houses, but about to accept an appointment at a church school in Maine. On May 8, she received a letter from George F. Degen of St. Catherine's Hall, a diocesan school for girls in Augusta, Maine acknowledging her application for a teaching position and, in effect, offering it to her. The prospect was far from tempting. The demand for art teaching, Degen explained, was very small and would be of an elementary character. The teacher appointed would be expected — dread words for any art or music teacher — to "fill in" with spelling, geography, arithmetic, etc. There was even worse to come. Because the school was relatively new, and because she would be "working for the church and not for gain," the salary would be a mere $20 monthly, with accommodation provided. Nell had heard of the position through the bishop's daughter, Bertha Miles, whom she had met at the Art Students Club and the Art Students League. Bertha had taught at St. Catherine's Hall but wanted to return to New York and wrote to Mrs. Newell to ask if Nell would be interested in replacing her. Nell accepted Degen's terms, and at the same time she wrote to her mother, justifying her decision. Her reasons were predictable: a regular salary, nearness to home, and for a devout churchgoer, the fact that it was a church school.

After three rewarding and successful years at Cooper, Nell's leave-taking in late May 1899 should have been joyful, but instead she left under what she felt was a cloud. Just before the end of the school year, a petition requesting longer studio hours circulated among the students. Nell had nothing to do with organizing the petition and, presumably because she was about to leave, nothing to do with framing the request. She felt, however, after a discussion with the organizers, that she had been largely responsible for the knowledge of its existence being kept from Miss Vinton. The petition, when made public, so irritated Miss Vinton that she wrote a long and detailed rebuttal. In taking her leave of Miss Vinton, Nell had not mentioned her involvement. In late May, filled with unease, she wrote to Miss Vinton from Boston, confessing to an error of judgement and ending with a poignant and moving appeal: "I am so unhappy about it all for although I may never go back to study at Cooper again, I love and respect you so much, Miss Vinton, that I cannot bear to think I may have lost your trust and confidence." Mary Vinton's reply was magnanimous. She exonerated Nell from any intention of wrongdoing and assured her of her unshaken belief in Nell's highmindedness. She also expressed her great regret that Nell would not be at the school the following year and offered this testimonial: "I shall miss you very much — for you are one of those in whom I feel I always may trust implicitly to do her duty in a perfectly simple and straightforward way and whose influence in the school is consequently invaluable to me." She asked Nell to extend her good wishes to Miss Graves, who had not been well, and to write to her with news of the school in Augusta.

Wilderness Years

Nell's role in the handling of the student petition may have blighted her perception of her final weeks at the Cooper Union, but her years there were halcyon ones. St. Catherine's Hall, on the other hand, was a catastrophe. Nell's misery can only be inferred in letters from the faithful Mary Gove. When Nell had been in residence for less than a month, Mary expressed sympathy for what she described as Nell's homesickness, but which was more likely a severe attack of angst, induced by an acute awareness of being in the wrong place with the wrong people. Unable to bear the thought of Nell living alone among unaccommodating strangers, Mary begged her not to write her such a "blue" letter again. Her next letter to Nell, written on October 16, was addressed to the house of Mrs A.C. Robinson of Massachusetts Avenue, Boston. Nell had bolted. She also seems to have recovered from the Augusta setback. Mary observed: "When you wrote to me last you seemed to be in excellent spirits. Under the same circumstances I would have utterly collapsed and probably had nervous prostration." She also alluded to a "beastly" set of people at St. Catherine's Hall, wondered how Nell had tolerated them for so long, and thought that she was perfectly justified in leaving. Mary, who was herself seldom downcast for long, offered that she was not unduly distressed by Nell's flight and expected that Nell would find something else soon. She then referred to what she, and others sub-sequently, regarded as Nell's proverbial luck: "The fates always seem kind to you and you generally get exactly what you want so I hope your customary good luck will not desert you."

It did not. Mary's next letter to Nell was to an address in Hamilton, Bermuda. Nell had found work as a governess or an au pair with Mr. and Mrs. H.K. White from Brookline, Massachusetts. The Whites, who had two children, wintered in Bermuda. Mary, understandably envious, wondered if in addition to wintering in Bermuda, Nell might also be going to the 1900 Paris Exposition, adding, "If you really want to go, I suppose with your usual good fortune a way will be provided." Nell did not go to Paris, but as an antidote to the trauma of St. Catherine's Hall and a respite from the "whirl" of New York, Bermuda was ideal. To her mother, she noted that the most exciting happening on the island was the scheduled arrival of the steamer from New York. Not even the weather could be relied upon for change: day after day of sunshine and equable temperatures, interrupted only by occasional wind and rain. The work, too, was quiet and system-atic. Mrs. White was well organized and the children, Louise and Bubs, were manageable. Nell felt perfectly well and with her penny-pinching New York days behind her, had developed a ravenous appetite. Exercising regularly and being outdoors with the children for a good part of each day, she feared she would be as "brown as an Indian" when she got home.

Bermuda was her first glimpse of a tropical setting. She reported seeing bamboo trees and fields of onion and arrowroot and, when driving with the Whites, woods where the narcissus grew wild and where the hedges of oleanders were so high she could scarcely see over the tops of them. But it was the subtle and varied greens and blues of the seawater and the creams and salmon pinks of the coral sands that caught her painter's eye. From a glass-bottomed boat she also saw corals and sea anemones, and she was taken to limestone caves draped with stalactites and stalagmites. She even found pleasant company. Miss Jones, a young woman of roughly her own age, had attended Grace Church in New York and taken tea in the Art Students

Club where she had met Mrs. Newell and Bertha Miles. Toward the end of the winter, Nell also sketched with a Miss Strange, who taught art and music at a school in Hamilton. Miss Strange had studied in New York and South Kensington and suggested that if Nell — who acknowledged that she badly needed the practice — returned the following winter, they should start a sketching club. Nell reported these and other details in letters written in pencil to save herself, as she put it, from falling into the hands of the *Beacon*: "I don't care to appear in print, thank you." A letter written in pencil presumably would have impressed an editor less than one written in ink.

For Nell, however, one winter in Bermuda was, as for Milton's pair in Eden, "paradise enow." By November 1900, she was back in St. Andrews having decided not to return to Bermuda with the Whites. Still unable to disregard the carrot of teaching, in September 1901, she took a job at the Halifax Ladies College in the capital city of Nova Scotia. If St. Catherine's Hall was a convulsion, Halifax Ladies College was an attenuated trauma. Mary Gove's letters again measure Nell's fortunes. In September 1902, within a few weeks of Nell's return for the new school year, Mary hoped that her letter found her better contented with things in general and regretted that there was "so much friction" at the college. Mary, impatient with Nell's low spirits, urged her to snap out of the state of "everlasting gloom" that Nell had admitted overshadowed her all the time. A month later, Mary was relieved to hear that Nell was getting interested in her classes and that parents had complimented her. That, she added, should keep her spirits up, as would the exhibitions, presumably of students' work, that Nell had organized. But by November, Nell was again out of sorts. Mary was sorry to hear that things had gone "agin" her again but assured Nell that life in Halifax could not be as dull as life in St. Andrews. Most of her interesting contemporaries had gone elsewhere, and there was not a single friend left of her own age. But no chiding from Mary could cure Nell. Teaching in a school did not suit her, and she was probably too controlling to settle quietly into the life of a closeted, if not exactly closed, community. In one of her letters, Mary offers a glimpse of what she obviously regarded as Nell's intransigence. After a disagreement with Mrs. Trueman, one of Nell's few friends at the college, Mary noted that Nell had settled the argument with one of her "little sermons." Mary noted that she herself had been subjected to these sermons but had not taken offence, even when Nell had made them personal.

In January 1903, Nell's spirits sank even lower when news reached her of the death of Augusta Graves after a lengthy illness. Augusta's death coincided with a particularly unpleasant period at the college. Nell and the principal did not get along. In February 1903, writing from Boston, where she had gone to look after an aged aunt and uncle, Mary sympathized with her loss of Augusta and regretted that Nell was again having such a hard time at the college. She provided no details but expostulated, "What an old bag the principle [*sic*] must be. How you must hate her." Later that same month, she again commiserated with Nell and hoped that she would remain at home next term, adding presciently that if St. Andrews became a place of importance, there might be openings for enterprising people like Nell. In March 1903, she urged Nell to stay home at the end of term as she couldn't bear to think of her "toiling away in that college that you loathe and despise, though you won't exactly acknowledge it." In April, however, the skies lifted a little, Mary referring to better days in store for the college, with "the people you dislike all leaving." But Nell was now thinking of New York for the following winter. Mary, who was still in Boston, asked her if she also would consider moving there so that they might be together. But she made no reference to the kind of work Nell had in mind except to say that New York would provide more opportunities. In her reply, Nell must have dismissed the possibility of Boston, Mary responding that "nothing but New York will do for you next winter."

Both Mary and Nell were in St. Andrews in July 1903, and the following September, Nell returned to the Halifax Ladies College, having shelved the idea of New York. The college had a new principal, and Mary noted that things were going more smoothly, even though Nell was still considering leaving for New York after the Christmas holidays. In a November letter, Mary noted that Nell had been giving public lectures again, a form of address that Nell clearly liked and to which she would return later in life. Mary's letters at this time are punctuated with references to books they were both reading: novels by Victor Hugo and Leo Tolstoy, and poetry by Dante Gabriel Rossetti. Mary expresses romantic longings and regrets that neither of them has married. With life easier at the college, Nell stayed on for another year, but she had no intention of becoming a fixture. In a letter from Bloemfontain, South Africa, written in November 1904, her cousin Alice Parker referred to Nell's plans for a business that depended on trustworthy people being found to manage the Beech Hill farm. George and Bella Mowat were now in their seventies. A letter addressed to Nell in early December from the Dairymen's Association of New Brunswick suggests that the scheme might have had some connection with dairying, but only the envelope has survived and the plans clearly never materialized.

Nell, presumably despairing of teaching and with no position to go to, left Halifax Ladies College in June 1905 and retreated to Beech Hill. Her luck had deserted her. In the winter of 1906/07 she contracted scarlet fever and in the months that followed, she suffered a nervous breakdown. She was thirty-one, unmarried, with no prospects, and no suitor in sight. In 1907, that was a kind of living death. The only concrete evidence of Nell's collapse is a reference, in a letter from her cousin Miriam Mowat, to a young woman who had "a nervous breakdown like yourself." The letter was addressed to the care of Mrs. William Dunbar in Cambridge, Massachusetts, where Nell seems to have gone for a rest cure. At the end of October she received a letter from Mary who was now back in St. Andrews and, at twenty-eight, preparing to marry. Her husband-to-be was William Carson, a St. Andrews man. Mary regretted that things were not as pleasant in Cambridge as Nell had anticipated but she was not surprised, as she had met a nurse in Boston who told "many strange tales" of Mrs. Dunbar. She did not elaborate, however. Nell had obviously shown distress in her last letter and had not kept a bargain with Mary: "Do you remember that you promised faithfully to see a doctor if you had one of those attacks again? From the tone of your last letter I should judge you did not keep your promise." At the same time, her cousin Miriam sent a similar exhortation:

> You just simply must not go on as you are doing,
> you must get well and you will not there where you
> are...Please! Please! drop it all and just give your
> whole attention to getting well. I have an awfully nice
> message from Mr. and Mrs. Hoar who say you must
> go at once to them just as soon as you can leave that
> Mrs. Dunbar. Tell her you are going to leave. Go this
> very minute. I presume she will want a weeks notice
> but don't stay a second longer...I know they will be
> so good to you and you can be quiet and just make up
> your mind to getting well...they are fond of you, very
> fond, don't wait any longer to see if things will be
> better. I wish we had never let you go. I think we were
> all mad.

By early January, Nell, who was feeling better, had heeded Mary and Miriam's advice and left the "horrid" Mrs. Dunbar's. "It is," wrote Mary, "a good thing that you left Mrs. Dunbar when you did or the consequences might have been serious." She followed this with a little homily: "If you look out for something to do again, do be guided a little in your choice by what your friends say." Miriam also expressed thanks that Nell, who was now staying with the Hoars in Brookline, had "had the sense to consult a doctor." By March 1908, Nell was well enough to take a job as an au pair with the Kennards of Beacon Street in Boston. Mary chided her for being " a very foolish little girl not to rest when you have the chance," but was delighted to hear that Nell was recovering her strength. She urged her to cut out bicycle riding, however, which she considered "not fit exercise for any woman." In June, Nell accompanied the Kennards to Cazenovia, New York, where she was well enough for Mary to write: "I am glad you like your work and that you are better. Your letter seemed quite like what you used to write before you were ill." By September the recovery was complete, Miriam writing: "You certainly are the limit. When I reach thirty perhaps I will have learned the gentle art of flirting like you my 'sweet inconsidcrate' cousin!" In spite of Miriam's reference to flirting and Nell's clearly romantic nature, there is no evidence that she ever had a suitor. When writing a novel that involved a romance, in her sixties, she confided to a friend that she had to watch movies in order to write the love parts.

Although returned to mental and physical health, Nell, now that she had only an au pair's income, had a new worry. How to keep Beech Hill? There is no record, but it seems likely that some of her teaching income had helped to pay the expenses of the farm. In a letter written in November 1908, Alice Parker referred to Nell's "home problems" and followed this with "I should think it would break your father's heart to lose Beech Hill." In the preceding twenty years George Mowat had been forced to raise cash by selling outlying fields, some to summer visitors who wanted to establish their own holiday houses. The original 150 acres was now a parcel of eighty acres overlooked by the farmhouse, barns, and gardens. Miriam's solution was for Nell to find a "nice rich man" to maintain both her and the farm, as it would be "a sin to leave the farm to any old person." In March 1909, Nell was still with the Kennards but had intimated to Mary that she would be home soon for a lengthy visit. She didn't specify a date, but her arrival was probably precipitated by an injury her mother sustained early in May. Bella Mowat fell, breaking her hip, and died from complications stemming from this injury at the end of May. She was seventy-nine years old.

A few months after Bella's death, Nell and her father decided that the farm, their only real asset, must be sold. George Mowat, who was now eighty-three, was too old for work, and Nell would not have been able to manage the farm on her own, even if she had been ready to stay home. On September 11, 1909, Beech Hill was sold to Mrs. Lucien Carr of Boston, who agreed to the unusual proviso that Nell and her father could continue to occupy the house and three surrounding acres for the remainder of their lives. It was a generous arrangement that probably extended George Mowat's life — he had known no other home — and assured him that Nell would always be housed. It was the best legacy he could manage. By March 1910, however, Nell, still restless, was in Palm Beach, Florida, serving as a governess with the Alonzo Zabriskie family. Her plan to stay with the Zabriskies through the following autumn drew a mild reproof from the usually tolerant Mary: "I hoped that now that the farm is sold...you would stay at home and be with your father but I suppose you would not be contented." At Palm Beach, Nell was in high spirits sending Mary a limerick which, judging by Mary's response, may have been slightly risqué. "Have you heard this," she asked:

> First pair of corsets, "I was pretty tight last night"
> Second pair, "Well I was on a pretty big bust myself."

"Not bad is it?" commented Mary.

The Making of Cottage Craft

Just how long Nell spent with the Zabriskies is not known. No letters have survived, either to or from her, between 1910 and 1914. The most likely explanation is that she returned home shortly after Mary's last known letter, written in March 1910. With the exception of her mother, Mary Gove (now Carson) was Nell's most faithful correspondent during this period, and the absence of letters may simply mean that Nell was now home at Beech Hill living with and looking after her father. Nell's own account, written many years later, of the years between her departure from Halifax

Nell, standing on right, at Beech Hill.

Ladies College and her return home is abrupt: "After leaving school [The Cooper Union], I spent several unprofitable years trying to teach art in a girls' boarding school, until some years later circumstances made it necessary for me to return to live at the farm." Whatever the date of Nell's return to Beech Hill, one fact is fairly certain: she and her father would have had to make do on the proceeds from the sale of the property and any savings Nell might have had. Summer boarders may have provided some income, but this alone would not have kept them over the winter.

The origins of Cottage Craft are similarly elided. Nell's description of the genesis of the business, published some twenty years later as an article, "Art as a Cash Crop," in the *Dalhousie Review*, has a mythic quality: "I started with a capital of $10.00: how I ever raised it, I don't know. I expended the entire amount in the purchase of some hooked rugs, that the country women made for me from my own designs. I was able to dispose of these rugs in Montreal at a little better price than I paid for them, which increased my capital to $15.00, and from that tiny germ an industry grew." In 1913, $10 would have been the equivalent of $200 now. What prompted Nell to approach the country women in the first place is never fully explained. In "Art as a Cash Crop," she attributes the impulse to a reaction against the design class at the Cooper Union:

> Every Saturday morning it was a custom for the students to attend a free lecture on art at the Metropolitan Museum. We would afterwards eat a meagre sandwich in the park and spend the afternoon exploring the Museum.
>
> On these occasions we were told by our instructors that we should start in the Egyptian room. They explained that in the decoration of a mummy case we would find the first primitive impulse of a race, unhampered by contact with our too standardized civilization. In short, we were to study the art of ancient Egypt as a scientist studies proto-plasm. It seemed that the ancient Egyptians could far surpass us; no one objected to their lack of perspective or their peculiar construction of figures; in fact, they had a freedom of expression that we poor students were denied and, most important of

all, their works of art sold for fabulous prices, while ours were of sadly little commercial value.

Now, while I liked Egypt in the museum, I despised it in the classroom. In the designing class, girls were made to work for days, often weeks, copying an Egyptian pattern. After that, they would be switched over to Assyria, and thence to Byzantium and Greece. I have no quarrel with historic ornament, it is a delightful study, but I still wonder why we were never asked to express something ourselves...I greatly enjoyed the return to country life and the friendship of my own people, with their kindly hospitality, their useful lives and the thrifty cheer of their homes, the rhythm of the country dance and the glory of the harvest, the peace of white quiet winters and the spring returning with mayflowers. Yet there were people who would say of me: "The poor girl! All her art education just thrown away!" Adding piteously, "and she studied in New York too!" . . .

The inspiration that I had brought back with me was not of New York but of Egypt. Here was I among my own people, again surrounded by the eternal beauty that was my heritage; here or nowhere could I establish a native art, an art that would express our own farm life so lovely and so little known. The art that would tell the story of the Maritimes must come from the people themselves, no one else could ever know; and then too we were so advantageouly remote from modern standardization, even as in ancient Egypt.

Missing from Nell's account is any reference — that those familiar with the development of design and the decorative arts at the turn of the twentieth century would expect to find — to a movement away from rule-bound academic design and, even more constraining, standardized industrial design, that had been going on for the previous twenty or thirty years. The Arts and Crafts movement, as it came to be known, originated in England toward the end of the nineteenth century, and by the early twentieth century, it had crossed the Atlantic to take root in New England and the eastern states. Its leading figure was William Morris, an inspired designer and social activist whose aim was to free industrial workers from numbing factory work, and society at large from cheap and often shoddy mass-produced goods. In industrial England, art and life had been sundered and Morris's millenarian aim was to reunite them. In Morris's workshops, handmade products would replace machine made ones. Design motifs would be taken from nature —plants, animals, and birds — and all products would be rendered in or upon natural materials such as wood, linen, clay, or copper.

Although she makes no references to the Arts and Crafts movement in her writings, Nell could hardly have been unaware of it during her student years in London and New York and even — though it may not have been in the mainstream of artistic and intellectual life — at Halifax Ladies College. Her view of Charlotte County's remoteness from "modern standardization," as an absolute advantage for the kind of products she had in mind, is the closest she came to acknowledging her debt to the Arts and Crafts movement. Like the author of that movement, there can be no doubt that for her a social purpose marched in step with the economic one. Nell needed an occupation and income, but she also saw herself as a crusader and benefactor. But whereas Morris looked to the liberation of urban workers, Nell looked to those in the country. Farm women were spared factory conditions and slums, but Nell's own experience had shown her that many of them lived difficult and restricted lives. A cottage handcraft industry would bring interest and variety to house-bound and sometimes isolated farm women, and it would inject ready money into a society that was often chronically short of it.

In her account of the making of Cottage Craft, Nell wrote as if the scheme was entirely of her own invention. But like most social movements, this one sprang from a general mood for change. There were parallel and even earlier developments in other parts of North America. The best documented, and possibly best known, was the

Sketch by Nell with the inscription, "This is the land where dwell the people who weave and spin." Courtesy of the Charlotte County Archives

Abnakee Rug Industry founded by Helen R. Albee in New Hampshire. Albee, a wealthy New Yorker skilled in textile design, decided to use her training to benefit the women of the country community in New Hampshire where she made her summer, and eventually her permanent, home. She chose the hooked rug, which was made in almost every household, and combining her knowledge of design, colour, and materials with the handcraft skills of her country neighbours, elevated this humble homemade product into an object of art that was sold first to summer residents and visitors, and then nationally. The poor may have preferred "boughten" goods that they did not have to make themselves and that were easy to clean and maintain, but the rich, nostalgic for the pre-industrial past, preferred the handmade.

In Charlotte County, the ideas of the Arts and Crafts movement, filtered through Nell, found receptive ground. The county had only recently passed out of the handcraft age. By 1860, most textiles for clothing, household, and decorative articles were made industrially and distributed to all parts of North America from manufacturing centres in Britain and New England. Spinning and hand weaving, which had once been practised in nearly every pioneer home, were almost lost arts that survived to the end of the century only in some rural areas. In New Brunswick, the lumber camps and fishing villages still required handwoven woollen cloth for heavy-duty clothing and blankets. The Dominion Census of 1871 recorded that among the 25,882 inhabitants of Charlotte County, 103 declared weaving as their occupation producing 22,692 yards of cloth. In addition to this, 47,128 yards of cloth was woven in the 1,109 ordinary households (almost 29 percent of the total 4,725 households) that reported cloth making for use in the home and, if there was a surplus, for sale or barter. (Some dry goods merchants would take homespun cloth, knitted socks, mittens, and other garments in exchange for goods.) The lumber trade, however, declined in the late 1870s, severely reducing the demand for workers, and clothing and blankets, in the camps. The census of 1881 showed a 36 percent drop in the production of homemade cloth. Spinning wheels and looms continued to be used in some rural homes as a matter of thrift, but by the last years of the century, most had been consigned to lofts and attics. Factory-made goods were more generally affordable and, in fact, prized. "Homemade," now a term of commendation, was then often used disparagingly. However, despite the appeal of factory made goods, many country women and their town sisters continued to find satisfaction in handwork. They knitted socks, mittens, and other garments for their families; embroidered tablecloths and cushion covers to bring a touch of colour and beauty to their homes; and hooked mats for their cold floors.

Hooked mats gave their makers the dual satisfaction of producing colourful, decorative home comforts from reused fabrics; creativity and thrift were combined. The still useable parts of worn woollen clothing and blankets were cut into narrow strips. A pattern, often a simple geometric one of circles drawn around a dinner plate, or squares obtained by careful measurement, was laid out on a burlap grain bag from the barn which had been unstitched to lie open and trimmed to the desired size. The strips of fabric, drawn through the spaces in the burlap mesh with a fine hook, formed closely packed loops on the upper side of the mat. The same technique could be used with spun and dyed wool yarn instead of fabric strips, and would have been almost as economical.

From girlhood, Nell had admired the hooked rugs in the kitchens of the farmhouses she visited. As an adult badly in need of income, she now saw them as a means whereby she and their makers might earn much-needed cash. She suspected that city-dwelling homemakers would be glad to buy them for their cheerful charm and utility, but like Helen Albee, she also realized that to make them truly attractive to discerning customers, good design would be a critical element. For that reason, the first three rugs she produced were hooked to designs that she sketched for the women who joined her in that 1913 experiment. Nell sent them to a Canadian handcrafts shop in Montreal where they sold quickly. Thus encouraged, over the next couple of years, Nell embarked on her full scheme: the development of a distinctive Charlotte County art that drew on native skill, native materials, and the natural beauty of the area. Tourists, as she would later note, could enjoy the latter for a brief season only: "We must therefore make for the fleeting tourist something that would forever be a reminder of our native land." Nell's vision for her craft workers is encapsulated in a stanza of poetry by Charles G.D. Roberts that she used as the frontispiece to her book *A Story of Cottage Craft*, compiled in 1958.

Make Thou my vision sane and clear
That I may see what beauty clings
In common forms and find the soul
Of unregarded things

In exhorting her craft workers to eschew the extraordinary she might also, consciously or unconsciously, have been reiterating advice impressed on her by Henry Twachtman many years earlier at the Cooper Union.

As a philosophical statement of intent, Charles G.D. Roberts's entreaty expressed the ideal, but Nell's knitters and weavers needed help in deciding which "common forms" might be marketable and how they might be applied to hooked rugs and embroidered bags and tablecloths. The farm and country women of Charlotte County had practical skills, but to these Nell added her acquired knowledge of good design, and they depended on her ability as a teacher to convey its principles.

Nell's first move was to commission the making of more hooked rugs. Groups of neighbouring workers, who usually gathered in one house, were instructed to choose subjects from the life and landscape around them. To guide them, she suggested subjects and approaches:

> When the cows come home at milking time...study all the lines and angles in the anatomy of a cow; observe the character of the head and the way the horns and ears [are]fitted on. Such details of all our farm animals must be memorized for future use.
>
> When [driving] through the country...notice the varying branches of the trees and the graceful outlines of the hills to give...a feeling for good lines. Then too...look for color harmony — patches of blue-green turnip fields set among fawn colored autumn stubble — gray barns with wide red granary doors — little white cottages sheltered by dense green fir woods. Endless combinations of color in wayside flowers, winter sunrises and evening light upon the hills.

Nell tried to elicit from her crafters what aspects of country or farm life most interested them, and when a crafter had an idea for a design Nell would talk it over with her and encourage her to make a sketch.

If the worker found a particular element too difficult to draw, then Nell would help by supplying a pencil drawing or a stencil of the object that could be fitted into the overall plan.

The results of her informal teaching of the fundamentals of design were so encouraging that Nell, as she later wrote, felt confident enough to lay down a few definite rules: "Nothing must be used in design that we are not familiar with in our everyday life — no lotus flowers, or birds of paradise... No designs should be copied from magazines or articles that our city friends brought us, nothing seen in shop windows or on the fancy work counters of department stores." She encouraged the crafters to "be constantly on the watch for something that would be completely their own." This general rule of original design became a guiding principle for the infant business. In the spring of 1914, Nell was able to buy $60 worth of rugs to sell during the summer.

Nell's stringent standards of design also applied to workmanship. Inez Lord, who worked as a forewoman for Cottage Craft in the forties and fifties, recalled that in order to get a job with Miss Mowat you had to live in Charlotte County and, having fulfilled that requirement, "you had to weave a pair of blankets for practice. If they were okay, then you could weave for Miss Mowat." Similar tests applied to all Cottage Craft products. No substandard work was bought and no experiment paid for until it had proved successful.

Because Nell's vision for Cottage Craft required the use of local materials, she had to have a ready supply of locally made wool yarn for her craft workers. A hand loom weaver working at full tilt can weave three yards of thirty-five-inch wide fabric in an hour, and might aim to produce ten to fifteen yards in a day. There were wool carding and spinning mills in the county, producing yarns in a limited range of natural and primary colours, and in the early years of Cottage Craft — from 1915 to 1919 — Nell must have used these, as well as small batches of handspun and vegetable-dyed wool. But as the demand for Cottage Craft products grew, more yarn and handwoven fabric were needed. And because she wanted the colours of her yarn to reflect the colours of the Charlotte County landscape Nell had to experiment

Nell, standing on right, with an
elderly spinner, circa 1915.

Courtesy of the Charlotte County Archives

with commercial chemical dyes and establish repeatable formulae for reproducing the colours she developed. She also needed space for treating large quantities of wool in various stages of preparation, and so by 1919, a wool processing shed, measuring about sixteen by twenty-five feet, was added to the back of the Beech Hill farmhouse.

To get around the county to buy wool and supply her crafters, Nell bought a car. She purchased wool in the fleece from Charlotte County farms. The rolling hill country was ideal for pasturage and the root crops, tolerant of the cool, humid climate and acidic soils, were ideal fodder. Sheep rearing, for mutton, lamb, and wool, was then encouraged by the provincial Department of Agriculture. Many years later, Frances Wren (1906-1990), a talented painter who worked for Nell from 1928 to 1942, described a typical wool gathering expedition: "I used to go with her in the spring in her 'tin lizzie' up through the country to collect the wool shorn off the sheep. The back seat of the car would be full of bags of wool; unwashed, full of hay, burdocks, etc. She also used to get wool from Deer Island. You could always recognize it because it was full of seaweed." Frances could have added that unwashed fleece, "in the grease" as it is sometimes called, smells strongly of lanolin, the natural oil that coats the fibres so a sheep remains dry and warm in any weather.

The journey itself was as memorable as the cargo. The *Beacon's* announcement, in its May 19, 1917, issue, "Miss Helen Mowat recently purchased an automobile," was an inadvertent warning to the townspeople. Nell was a notoriously bad driver. St. Andrews folklore has Nell, when she first acquired her car, driving to St. Stephen. When she got there she couldn't remember how to stop so she turned around and drove all the way back to St. Andrews. Unless challenged, according to Alexie Smith, she occupied the middle of the road and "thought nothing of turning her head right round to talk to you in the back seat while she was driving." Alexie's mother, Jennie Hare, worked for Nell and as a girl, Alexie accompanied Nell on yarn deliveries to her crafters. Myrtis Roach, who as a child occasionally rode in the rumble seat of Nell's coupe, recalled that she drove "ramrod straight, with a proper little hat, dress and coat." Myrtis never saw Nell without a hat that she always wore slightly tilted. In December 1922, all traffic in New Brunswick was officially moved to the right of the road but the switch, even if registered by Nell, unlikely affected her driving. Her car was so often in the ditch that a remark by Charlie Kelly, a local handyman and driver, became a town aphorism: "You can't come to town but what Lily's on the road or Nellie's off it!" Another version has Charlie spending "a lot of time picking Lily up off the road and putting Grace Helen back on it." (Lily Mowat, a distant cousin to Nell, lived in Chamcook and often walked the few miles into town to her work as bookkeeper in G.K. Greenlaw's store and to all hockey games; she was an ardent fan.)

In 1935, Nell and Martin L Parker, also a resident of St. Andrews, had identical cars, Ford V-8 roadsters with rumble seats, both of a sandy beige colour. Martin Parker's daughter Nina Parker (now Needler) knew which of them was driving down Montague Street toward her home because Miss Mowat always drove right down the *middle* of the road. Another idiosyncrasy was her refusal to use the car heater. She regarded it as sissy. As a boy, Basil Lowery, whose mother, Phoebe, was both a housekeeper and weaver for Nell, learned two things when driving with Miss Mowat in winter: one, dress warmly; and two, take an interior windshield scraping tool of some kind. To keep herself warm, Nell wore a big black fur coat and to warm her feet, she carried hot bricks. Nell continued to drive until she was eighty, continuing even after a mishap a few years earlier at

Charlie Taylor's garage blackened her eye. She said to Basil, "You remember the story in the Bible of Lot's wife who looked back and was turned into a block of salt. Well I looked back and turned into a lamp post."

Once the raw wool had been brought back to Beech Hill, the first task was to remove all the lanolin and dirt. In the wool industry, the process is called scouring, a word whose harsh sound indicates how thorough the washing must be to enable the wool fibres to take up the dye evenly. For the washing and rinsing, a plentiful supply of soft water was vital; hard water contains minerals that might combine chemically with soap to coat the fibres. Due to the seasonal drying out of its well, Beech Hill had experienced a long struggle with its water supply, so when a kitchen was added to the back of the house in the middle of the nineteenth century, a large brick cistern was built below it for storing rainwater from the roof. Next to melted snow, rainwater is the softest water obtainable. Later, a large metal tank was installed in the attic above the kitchen. Water from the cellar cistern could then be pumped up into the tank to provide gravity-fed rainwater whenever it was needed in the house or in the new wool shed. In dry years, when rainfall was insufficient, there was an alternative water supply close at hand. Since 1889, St. Andrews has been blessed with good soft water from Chamcook Lake. The supply line to the town passed near Beech Hill farm and a feeder surface line to the farm guaranteed a regular supply. There was no danger of freezing because the preparation of the wool was a summer activity; some of the steps in the process could only be carried on outdoors, and a supply of yarn was needed by the crafters for winter work.

After the wool had been washed, rinsed, and partially dried, the next step was to immerse it in a dye bath set up on the lawn, east of the house. The bath was a copper pot, about four feet in diameter that had been brought by Loyalist settlers around 1783. It was set into a brick box about eight feet square built in such a way that a wood fire could be made and tended beneath it. The dye bath was heated to just below the boiling point and the temperature maintained for up to an hour. Dyeing is an exacting procedure, requiring precise measurement of the dye powder itself and of the mordant (in this case dilute sulphuric acid) which fixes, or makes "fast," the colour to the fibre. The amount of water used to make up the dye bath, the amount of wool to be dyed, and the temperature of the bath, especially at the point when the material is immersed, had to be carefully monitored. To protect legs and trousers from the dilute sulphuric acid, the dyer wore knee-length leggings that were tied on, and to ensure even dyeing, he wielded a large wooden paddle with which he constantly stirred and lifted the wool.

To dry, the dyed wool was spread on large racks of chicken wire stretched on wooden frames. These were usually set up on trestles outdoors where warm breezes could move freely through the locks of wool. In persistently wet weather, however, the racks were moved indoors to an old stone milk house, which stood near the kitchen door behind the house. When thoroughly dry, the wool was bundled up and taken to St. Stephen, fifteen miles away, for carding and spinning, the next steps in the process.

John Speedy and Thomas Davidson built the Speedy and Davidson Woolen Mill on King Street, St. Stephen, in 1913, on a site now occupied by a Kent building supplies store. At the mill, a carding machine teased the tangled fibres into a fluffy, loose mass of uniform width and thickness. From that mass, narrow bands were separated and lightly twisted into rovings that were fed onto the bobbins of a spinning machine. The bobbins drew out the rovings into single yarns. Yarn intended for the warp, that is the closely arranged strands set on the loom as the foundation threads for the weaving, were given a tight, hard twist and wound onto large cones that would hold a continuous length of up to 1,700 yards. Weft yarn, which the weaver would throw back and forth across the warp in a shuttle, had a softer twist and was also wound onto cones. Yarn intended for knitting also had a soft twist, and was made up into skeins weighing about four ounces of either single ply for lightweight garments or two ply for heavier ones.

Once ready, the spun yarn was collected and brought back to Beech Hill for further treatment. Skeined knitting yarn was washed again to soften it and then hung out to dry. Batches of knitting and weaving yarns in all colours were then made up and Nell would set out to deliver them to the farm supply depots of the Cottage Craft forewomen. Frances Wren, who often helped Nell with the deliveries in the late twenties, thirties, and early forties, has fond memories of the farmhouse kitchens: "We were often asked to have supper at farmhouses, in big warm kitchens; big tables, lots of home-cooked food, and many people — family and farm hands. There was a very nice friendly, warm, comfortable atmosphere in those farmhouse kitchens. One I remember in particular, was the farm of Mr. and Mrs. Tilley Reed at Lever Settlement." These occasions and rooms meant a great deal to Nell. She was an extremely convivial woman, and the country kitchens, which in contrast to stiff "best parlours," were decorated colourfully and informally, reassured her that Charlotte County farm women were ideal instruments for giving form and substance to her vision of Cottage Craft.

From the upcountry looms, the handwoven cloth was brought back again to Beech Hill in twenty-five-yard lengths or "webs" for washing and "fulling." Fulling, or milling, the cloth had the effect of slightly felting it, shrinking the width and length but increasing its density. Boyd Merrill, who was Nell's production manager and right-hand man after 1925, was working one day at the fulling machine when a journalist from *Canadian Home Journal* came and asked if he could be shown what went on in the woolshed. Giving credit where it was due, Boyd explained that the workers at Cottage Craft had learned the art of fulling from "an old man who understood milling and fulling as no one else hereabouts did. He showed us how to build the box and how to treat the cloth. Before that, the homespun wouldn't keep its shape, it would bag and wrinkle, now when it comes from the fulling there is no danger of that." Unfortunately, the name and story of that invaluable old man was never recorded, but it is most likely that he had worked in the woollen industry in Britain before he came to Charlotte County. His magic machine and the general enterprise at Beech Hill impressed the journalist, who wrote: "Even the fulling-machine, they have made themselves, shaped the rollers from the trees that grow all about them, built the big cram-box, in which the web is placed to

Bolts of homespun cloth. Courtesy of the Charlotte County Archives

be rolled and churned and kneaded and pounded. About twenty-five yards of cloth go into the fulling-box, and the cloth is whirled about, the rollers driven by a belt from a gas-engine, making two hundred revolutions a minute, for two hours, until shrunken to the wanted width." This graphic description needs only a few more details to be complete: the fulling machine itself was made of wood and was about six feet tall, three feet wide, and ten or twelve feet long. The two ends of the web were sewn together to form a continuous loop that passed around the two interior wooden rollers, which were two to three feet in diameter. The rollers prevented the web from becoming impossibly tangled by the pommelling in what was only a couple of feet of soapy water. Andy Leighton (a great grandson of Mrs. Lucien Carr) whose family owns Beech Hill farm, has a vivid childhood memory of the woolshed as "crowded, dark, wet, slippery and [it] smelled of wet wool and soap." After rinsing, the web was removed from the fulling machine, put through a large wringer and taken outdoors where it was stretched out on wood-framed racks to dry.

The reward for this prodigious effort, as one early commentator noted, was the faithful reproduction of the colours of the New Brunswick countryside: "the green of the spruce trees, the purple of the blueberries, the yellow of the goldenrod, and the bright blue of New Brunswick's lakes and coastal waters... Homespun vegetable dyes are responsible for the soft, harmonious and distinctive colours of Cottage Craft tweed. One of Miss Mowat's basic tenets — to follow nature's colours has proven successful." When, as an adult, Basil Lowery questioned Nell about her choice of regional names for the Cottage Craft colours, she replied feelingly, "because it was the part of the world I loved the most."

When the indispensable Boyd Merrill wasn't busy with wool preparation, or fulling, or engine maintenance, or pickups and deliveries, he might be found tending the vegetable and flower gardens at Beech Hill, or helping a weaver upcountry to string up her loom. He was everywhere and anywhere he was needed, often in the summer being "helped" by two or three children, who all remember his patience and good humour. Basil Lowery, has two especially clear memories of times spent with Boyd in the woolshed. Once when Basil's childish gaze was fixed on the big cigar Boyd was smoking, Boyd offered him a puff. Basil gravely accepted and was so thoroughly sick that he has never smoked again. On another occasion, when he was sitting near the one-stroke engine, watching Boyd at work, he suddenly fainted away and the next thing he knew he was being brought round by Nell and a teaspoonful of brandy in the house. He'd been overcome by carbon monoxide from that workhorse engine. The three Leighton children, Polly, Andy, and Tim, summered at Beech Hill starting in 1935 when their parents built their own house on the property bought by their great-grandmother Mrs. Lucien Carr in 1909. They also spent time with Boyd in the woolshed and the garden, joining in whatever activity was on offer in the way children do on long summer days. When talking about Boyd Merrill now, Andy Leighton's discourse is laced with superlatives: "a fantastic mechanic," "a superb weaver," "flawless stuff . . ."

After the crowded days of spring and summer, when the annual supply of dyed and spun wool was prepared, Boyd Merrill sat down at his own loom in the quiet of fall and winter. Boyd grew up at De Wolfe near Moore's Mills and had learned to weave in his family

Nell seated, with book, in a log cabin on the Beech Hill property.
Courtesy of the Charlotte County Archives

home. He also knew how to knit, having been taught by his mother while he was quarantined with scarlet fever as a boy. His knowledge of how to prepare and dye raw wool and how to weave and knit the spun yarn were invaluable assets, but equally important to life at Beech Hill was his warm, friendly nature. He met and married Helen McKinney of Elmsville when they were both working at Clibrig, the farm next to Beech Hill, and in 1925 they had a daughter, Madeline (nicknamed Mady). Both he and Helen wove for Cottage Craft during their association with the business, and Mady learned to weave at their knees. The Merrills lived at Beech Hill from 1925 until about 1933 when they moved to St. Andrews so that Helen could operate her own business for summer tourists, Merrill's Cabins on Reed Avenue. Boyd, however, continued to work with Nell and when gasoline rationing during World War II drastically reduced the number of summer tourists, the family returned to live at the farm for a year.

Pencil sketch by Nell of a mother and child in the
Beech Hill kitchen. Courtesy of the Charlotte County Archives

A Shop by the Side of the Road

As well as a pool of skilled handcraft workers nearby, St. Andrews had the second prerequisite for a successful cottage industry. All her life Nell had been accustomed to the migration of summer people who came by rail to vacation at the Beech Hill farm and other boarding houses, or at one of the large hotels built to accommodate them. As an attractive, if somewhat dilapidated, old town, kept temperate and virtually mosquito free in summer by the cool waters of Passamaquoddy Bay, St. Andrews was a magnet for well-to-do city dwellers from Quebec, Ontario, and New England. In 1903, the Canadian Pacific Railway had bought the town's largest hotel, the Algonquin, drawing St. Andrews into the orbit of its powerful advertising department. In addition to vacationers, more than twenty families arrived annually to take up residence in their own summer homes in or near the town. Prominent among them was Sir William Van Horne, builder of the CPR, who arrived in his own private railway car at his own little station on the shore just below Beech Hill. From there he crossed by horse carriage or motor launch, depending on the level of the tide, to his estate on Minister's Island. In effect, the customers for Nell's fledgling enterprise came to town in summer shoals, and she and her craft workers used their long, less busy winter hours making a net of attractive products with which to seine the tourist waters.

The Beech Hill farmhouse had two parlours, one on either side of the large front entry hall. Nell set up the one on the roadside of the house as a shop, displaying the locally made hooked rugs, and let it be known to the summer community that she was open for business. As well as the rugs, she displayed homespun yard goods that she had bought in Quebec with part of the profit from the initial rug venture. This was one of her most prescient steps because not only did the Quebec goods attract customers but they demonstrated to her crafters that they themselves were capable of work that was just as good. Spinning wheels and looms were removed from sheds and attics, twenty or thirty years of dust cleaned away, and their whirring and thumping was heard again in households throughout Charlotte County. Homespun yarn and handwoven fabric would become the signature products of the business. But in these early experimental days, all forms of handwork with threads, yarns, and woven fabric were being explored by a growing cohort of workers. An early success was handbags for women, made of woven homespun fabric, which was then decorated with coloured yarns applied by various needlework techniques.

The *St. Andrews Beacon* helped greatly with promotion of the fledgling business. Robert Armstrong, editor from 1889 to 1914, had been an ally of Nell's since she was a girl, publishing her descriptions of the sights of London and regularly noting her homecomings and doings during her student and teaching years in the social column. Wallace Broad, editor from 1914 until publication ceased in 1919, continued the *Beacon's* interest in Nell. Thanks to him, we now have several notices about Cottage Craft in its early years.

The year 1917 was a crowded one, and fateful in that it opened and closed with deaths that would affect Nell and her workers. In mid-April, Nell's father George died after a sudden decline at ninety-one years. So it was not until late June that a paragraph in the local and general column of the *Beacon* announced that "Charlotte County Crafts exhibits, under the management of Miss G. Helen Mowat, will reopen on Monday, June 25, for the 1917 season. All are cordially invited to inspect the work...at Beech Hill...Many novelties have been made, and much beautiful work has been done by the cottagers during the past winter." Then a wonderfully detailed report appeared on July 21, 1917, a full column in length, telling a little about the history of the business, and giving a lively description of the goods on display:

On the St. John road half a mile from St. Andrews, lies Beech Hill, the cradle of Cottage Craft. There four years ago a modest beginning in the home industries was made by Miss Helen Mowat...From a small start Miss Mowat now has more than seventy workers. She has branches...all over the county...The other day I visited the Cottage Craft Shop at Beech Hill and examined the work for the year.

The first thing I noticed was the pile of rugs, both hooked and woven. There were many designs, roosters, bunches of flowers, ducks, fruit, winter scenes. The two that I admired most were a yachting scene, and a typical farm scene — a little house and a big barn.

The bags, the idea for which originated with Miss Edith Townsend, are rainbow-hued, some are woven with bright wools; others have crocheted flowers and berries applied; while most fascinating are the ones with embroidered pictures; one with a flock of chickens, another with a country village, a third an old fisherman rowing out to his weir. The most attractive was a farmhouse interior where an old couple sat winding wool, on the floor was a braided rug, a bird hung in a cage, geraniums were on the window sill, and on the wall was the motto "Bless Our Home."

On one table I saw two bed spreads that were really lovely. One was knit, the other crocheted. Beside them were the toys. Of these I shall mention only the block villages. In each box are ten pieces, houses, barns, a church and a school house. These were made by the country children during the long winter evenings on the farm…The corsage bouquets of colored wool were also very pretty.

The author, most likely Freda Wren (the article is signed with the initials "F.W.") singled out, as quintessential Charlotte County products, luncheon napkins and a tablecloth made by Helen Gilman of Bartlett's Mills. Each napkin was embroidered with a different Charlotte County country scene: a farm in winter, a sunset, a farmer herding sheep. The embroidered tablecloth represented the Charlotte County Fair, two edges showing the road leading to the fair and the centre, the fairgrounds themselves — a balky cow, prize pigs, crated hens, a soft drink stand, the whole "a miracle of design."

This account in the *Beacon* shows how quickly the craft workers had learned to develop their own designs, and how equally quickly Cottage Craft had become an established business. To coordinate the work of seventy outworkers and keep them supplied with raw materials meant that Nell had to become an executive. She had already found it necessary to employ a secretary (Jennie Hare) in 1916 and to designate several forewomen. As well as distributing yarn to farms throughout the county, these forewomen acted as interim consultants on the handworked goods, and collected and brought the finished items to the Beech Hill shop. Their farms were the "branches" referred to in the newspaper report.

Three months later, a subsequent report in the *Beacon* informed readers that on the afternoon of October 18, 1917, "Miss Nellie Mowat entertained the heads of the different departments of the Cottage Craft at her home 'Beech Hill.'" The reporter then named all the women who attended, and because it is the only known list of Nell's early craft collaborators, it is appropriate to reproduce it here. Their names were arranged according to the mainly rural settlements where they lived and maintained outlying Cottage Craft depots, and in the case of married women, the author observed the then polite rule of using their husbands', not their own given, names:

Waweig	Rollingdam	Bayside
Miss Alice Nixon	Miss Bertha Richardson	Mrs. David McLaughlin
Mrs. Warren Bartlett	Miss Jessie Boyd	Mrs. August Greenlaw
Miss Winnifred Thomas		Miss Marion Greenlaw
Miss Thelma Thomas	Bartlett's Mills	
	Miss Helen Gilman	

Chamcook	St. Andrews	
Miss Edith Townsend	Mrs. Patrick Parker	Miss Georgie Carson
Miss Ruby Rankine	Mrs. W. Hare	Miss Freda Wren
Mrs. Lawrence Parker	Mrs. W. Carson	Miss Jennie Trusdell
Mrs. John Scullion	[née Mary Gove]	Miss Bessie Thompson

This was effectively a staff meeting at which the boss reviewed achievements since the last meeting and reiterated the aims of the business and the standards expected of its workers. The following are some of the key passages and phrases in the reporter's account of Nell's talk: "Now in one day when she goes through the country she buys up two hundred dollars' worth of rugs, bags, etc....orders come from every state. Every day large stores write for samples...work has grown so greatly that the heads of departments must look after their workers...train themselves to see harmony...nature is the best guide...Above all there must be careful workmanship... each piece must have character...must be perfect to be saleable." In a motivational conclusion, Nell singled out two pieces of work that had been acquired by museums. One was a rug, hooked by Mrs. John Morrison, of good colours, bright but in harmony. The other was the county fair tablecloth, embroidered by Miss Helen Gilman. Nell described it as a "winter's work, original, distinctive of Charlotte County, signed by the maker." And she left the assembled workers with this thought: "To be expert, the workers must always be alert to see what in nature can be used. They must work with their minds as well as with their hands to take the beauty of Charlotte County to send into the world."

Unfortunately, no list remains of the more than seventy crafters throughout the county who were plying their needles, hooks, and shuttles to produce the distinctive Cottage Craft goods. Most of the earliest records, which would have contained lists of workers, did not survive the several moves during the evolution of the business. Nell would have made lists as would have her secretary Jennie Hare (whose name appears as Mrs. W. Hare in the lists above).

Jennie was the daughter of Charles Horsnell, a St. Andrews stone-mason. After she graduated from the Charlotte County Grammar School in 1907, Jennie went to work in Saint John and there met William S. Hare. The couple married in early 1914 and decided to "go West," settling in Winnipeg where their daughter Alexie was born in November 1915. William worked as a demonstrator for the Nobel's explosives company so it was probably inevitable that he would enlist, which he did in 1915, as soon as Jennie was safely delivered of Alexie. When he left for service overseas, Jennie brought six-month-old Alexie back to St. Andrews for the duration of the war. Soon after their return, Jennie began work as Nell's secretary and she and baby Alexie went to live at Beech Hill with Nell, then aged forty, and her father George, eighty-nine. So it was to Beech Hill that Jennie's father came just seven weeks after the October staff meeting, on December 6, 1917, with the news that her husband, William Hare, had been killed in the war overseas. As it happened, this was also the day of the devastating munitions ship explosion in Halifax harbour. The year 1917 came to a very grim close. But there were crafters who needed supplies of yarn and fabric for their winter's work, mail orders to be attended to, plans to be made — in short, work to be done while heavy hearts mended.

The remarkable success of Cottage Craft, from its very beginning, exerted pressures on both Nell and Beech Hill. With retailing at the front of the farmhouse and wool processing at the back, Nell felt squeezed out of house and home. The front parlour soon proved inadequate for the summer retail business and enforced a move. Under the stress of a rapidly growing business, Nell suffered a recurrence of the nervous complaint that afflicted her in her last years

Watercolour by Nell of interior of Beech Hill.
Courtesy of Anthony E. Hilditch

of teaching. In 1919, her cousin Miriam Mowat Everett, who had grown up at Beech Hill, came to her aid, first as joint manager, then as a partner when the business was legally registered as Charlotte County Cottage Craft early in 1920. Although Miriam was nine years younger, she and Nell were, in effect, sisters, so while her recently demobilized husband, Herbert Everett, studied medicine at McGill, Miriam and her baby daughter spent the summer of 1919 with Nell at Beech Hill.

The reporter for the *Beacon* noted, when announcing the move to a new shop in June 1919, that "visitors will miss the visit to Miss Mowat's charming home on Beech Hill, yet they will find the new Cottage Craft easier to reach." The new shop was set up in a rented three-storey building on the main street of St. Andrews, formerly occupied by a men's clothing store owned and operated by R.A. Stuart, high sheriff of Charlotte County (now the Leather House). Again we have the reporter for the *Beacon* to thank for a very informative description of the new Cottage Craft: "the two large front windows displayed handmade rugs draped around a spinning wheel, one having a large fruit-basket design hooked into a black background, and two bedspreads, one of rose colour and one of blue, each embroidered with white wool. There was also a woven rag rug in a hit-or-miss pattern (that is, the colours woven in randomly). Inside the shop were "a very large assortment of homespun" yard goods and "the ever popular homespun blankets," as well as the handbags made of homespun and embroidered in "all the old favorite" designs such as the delicately coloured butterfly design, and a new thistle design. New products for this season were blankets woven especially for babies and then embroidered with designs such as a band of pale blue butterflies or a wreath of apple blossoms. The reporter also remarked on trays painted with winter scenes, an embroidered blue linen bridge cloth and napkins, and some rose-coloured beads. The beads may have been made by Mary Gove Carson, Nell Mowat's longtime friend and now her chief liason worker with crafters who lived in town. (In his 1933 article for *Canadian Home Journal*, Louis Arthur Cuningham wrote of a crafter "gathering the little sea shells and tinting and stringing them." Mary's niece, Georgina Gove Doyle, remembers her aunt using small shells in craft work.)

The *Beacon* reporter also wrote this intriguing paragraph: "The trench coats this year show the new embroidery and are really prettier than before. There is one of white edged with black and finishes [*sic*] with a band of dull pink and blue. To match this there is a small bag with cord and tassel and a larger shopping bag." The description is puzzling because the term "trench coat" now usually refers to a waterproof, belted overcoat of military style with buttoned straps at the shoulders and wrists. A garment offered by Cottage Craft would certainly have been made of handwoven wool, or homespun as it was commonly called, so it would not have been waterproof and it is very unlikely that it would have had a strongly military style. Nell, an imperialist, was an ardent supporter of the war but she would not have approved a fad or fashion stemming from it in a Cottage Craft product. Perhaps after World War I "trench coat" was used rather loosely for a while to indicate simply an overcoat.

The shop lasted at this Water Street location for one season

Watercolour by Nell of the entrance hall at Beech Hill.
Jamie Steele (Courtesy of Anthony E. Hilditch)

only because Nell's imagination was fully occupied with ideas for expanding the business and she needed still more space. Cottage Craft was doing extremely well. In 1920, six years after she started, Nell grossed $40,406.09 (from the sale of knit bags, wool, and hooked rugs), from which she declared a net profit of $10,075.77. No small sum at the time. That year she paid taxes of $615.02. Despite the return of her nervous complaint, she now had the confidence to forge ahead, and in April 1920, she bought a large prominent red brick house in St. Andrews. Chestnut Hall, for which she paid $5,750, is a neoclassical building constructed in 1824, that stands at the corner of King and Montague Streets, two blocks, or a pleasant stroll, from the business centre on Water Street. King is the town's show street and its main north-south axis. Until Nell bought the house, it had been a family home. With its geometrical arrangement of windows and

Chestnut Hall. Courtesy of the Charlotte County Archives

strong vertical lines, it provided a more formal setting than the term "cottage craft" implies, but the house benefited from the softening lines and shade of the large elm trees that then stood around it, and its central door, although elevated, had a cheerful fanlight and generous sidelights. Inside, a welcoming entry hall showed off a pretty curved staircase, and, to the right, a drawing-room and dining room, each of fair size, opened onto each other through a wide doorway. On the left of the entry hall was another parlour that the business could use. Almost as important as the ground floor rooms was the capacious basement, with its own kitchen and fireplace, that Nell immediately earmarked as a prospective workshop for further craft ventures. The four second-floor bedrooms might have seemed an incidental bonus, but she intended to occupy one of them herself during the tourist season and rent the remaining three to summer people. The fineness and solidity of Chestnut Hall would have pleased Nell, but more than this, they signaled that Charlotte County Cottage Craft had moved out of the experimental into the established phase.

With the help of Jennie Hare and Miriam Everett and others, the retail shop and office were set up in the former drawing-room and dining room. Another room, possibly the other parlour, was made into a tea room for customers. Jennie had become more of an executive assistant than a secretary and because both she and Miriam were mothers of young children, neither was likely able to work full-time. As a result, in 1919, Nell hired Dorothy Wisely, a young woman from Lincoln, near Fredericton, to combine the jobs of private secretary and shop clerk. It was the beginning of a long association with Cottage Craft that lasted until 1946. Dorothy met and married a young St. Andrews man, William Thompson, and they raised two children, Robert and Joyce. Other staff at the new location in Chestnut Hall included Mr. and Mrs. Cleve Mitchell, a young couple with a baby son, who in summer lived in an ell at the back of the house; in winter, they moved into the warmer main house. Cleve acted as the general handyman, looking after the building and grounds, and the wood and coal and firing, while Mrs. Mitchell did the housekeeping and cooking.

Once the business had settled into its new quarters, its second upheaval in two years, Nell was persuaded to take a rest. There must have been enough stock in hand for the summer trade, and staff in whom she had confidence, because in mid-July 1920 she took a summer voyage to England, sailing from Montreal on July 10. For the proprietor of a summer business this was a remarkable step — and a measure of her need for rest and relaxation. The trip had the desired effect: not only was Nell's equilibrium restored but she was fired with fresh enthusiasm for two more projects that had been germinating in her mind for several years.

Pottery and Linen

For a single woman starting out with very little capital, a success-ful cottage industry producing woollen goods might have seemed a sufficient achievement, but from the outset, Nell had harboured a larger vision for the town and the county. While acknowledging that tourism was St. Andrews' bread and butter, she disliked the town's dependence on it and, as a corollary of this, the suffix "St. Andrews-by-the Sea," coined and promoted by the advertising division of the CPR. Places should stick to the names they were given, she com-mented in a 1924 interview (for an article in *Maclean's*) with Norman Rankin, a publicist for the CPR. In that same interview she remarked that while she wanted old traditions, names, and customs retained, she also wanted Charlotte County to progress materially through the manufacture of local raw materials. She had in mind enterprises such as the canning of fish, fruit, and vegetables; the making of pottery; the growing of flax and the manufacture of linen. "I see a wonderful future for this part of the world," she asserted. "We have fine quality clays — I'd like to see a pottery industry established; we can grow flax — I'd like to see the flax industry developed; the farm-ers can and would produce it if encouragement is offered. They have so little and so restricted a market. They don't try to get rich; they put home and family happiness first."

The refrain of economic development through small-scale industry was one taken up periodically by the *St. Andrews Beacon*. The newspaper's suggestions were boat and yacht building, a cooperage for making fish barrels, and handcraft industries of the kind found in the town's Scottish namesake: golf clubs, tennis rackets, and fishing rods. Small handcraft industries, the *Beacon* proclaimed in July 1918, would neither deface the town nor offend the rich summer visitors who, on their return to the cities of the eastern seaboard, would carry word of the town's products — the most effective kind of advertising. For the *Beacon*, Nell and Cottage Craft were standard bearers for the new economy and whenever possible the paper shone its spotlight upon them.

First on Nell's list for a broader economic base was a pottery. As a girl she had amused herself by making marbles from the red clay that outcrops along the seashore at St. Andrews. From marbles to saleable pots was, for the ambitious entrepreneur that she had now become, a small step. Not only this, but a pottery fitted neatly within the Cottage Craft philosophy, and its products could be presented sympathetically with the textiles already on offer. In her travels around England in 1920, Nell visited with several second cousins who had moved from St. Andrews to work or retire in the milder English climate. Among them was Annie Parker, widow of Dr. Neville Parker, daughter-in-law to Nell's great aunt Eliza and mother of her childhood friend Alice Parker. The Parkers had settled in Bovey Tracey in Devon, a picturesque village on the edge of Dartmoor that was well-known for making decorative pottery. The village lies in a basin of clays deposited during the Eocene by the erosion of nearby Dartmoor. Here Nell met a potter, Bernard Kane, whose work she admired. She promptly placed an order with him for a cup and saucer that incorporated a decorative theme of her own. When it turned out well, she ordered five dozen more for use in her Cottage Craft tea room in St. Andrews. In the course of the transaction, Nell must have consulted him about how she should go about establishing a pottery and before she left England, she also must have planted the idea of him and his family coming to Canada and starting a pottery with her under the Cottage Craft banner.

Nell sailed for home in mid-September, having promised to send samples of local clay to England for Bernard Kane to shape and test in his kiln. The availability of an adequate supply of clay with the right properties for ceramic work, either in St. Andrews or Charlotte County, was a fundamental requirement. To meet Nell's high standard, a Cottage Craft product had to literally spring from the very earth of the region and be worked on by the mind and hands of one of its daughters or sons. Only then

Bernard Kane.
Courtesy of the Charlotte County Archives

could it be offered proudly, "the beauty," as she put it, "of Charlotte County going out into the world." If there was no suitable clay, the pottery project would not be undertaken.

In the months following her return to St. Andrews, Nell quizzed everyone she knew about sources of clay and talked to several businessmen who were optimistic about the prospects for raising capital for a pottery. In late October, she mailed Bernard Kane samples of red and grey clay of which, she noted, there was "an unlimited supply... the [grey] granite is found at St. George, a place 20 miles from here...I shall anxiously wait for your verdict, for if you offer any encouragement at all, I intend to start my pottery in the spring, provided I can persuade you to come over to go into it with me."

While awaiting Bernard Kane's all-important verdict, Nell helped with the dispatch of an exceptionally heavy flurry of Christmas mail orders and considered her next move on another project she hoped to initiate. During the first half of the nineteenth century, societies for the production of flax and hemp could be found across the country. New Brunswick soils were noted for their suitability, and in 1871, according to the census of that year, provincial weavers produced 74,000 yards of linen. By 1891, production, under pressure from cheaper machine-produced products, had fallen to 25,000 yards. Nell intended to revive the flax industry, if not of New Brunswick, then of Charlotte County.

As early as April 1917, she had sent an inquiry to the Dominion Department of Agriculture in Ottawa, asking about the suitability of Charlotte County for the venture. The reply from the chief of the Division of Economic Fibre Production, G.G. Bramhill, was extremely encouraging. The supply of flax fibre had been much reduced by the war in Europe, so that the price paid for fibre was very high, and in Mr. Bramhill's opinion, the summer climate of Charlotte County was enough like Ireland's to ensure that a crop would thrive. Yield would, of course, depend on the suitability of the soils. He did not mention that flax had been grown successfully in the southeast of the province and, in all likelihood, was still being grown in the northeast.

In Westmorland County, an area that embraces Moncton, Shediac, Dorchester, and Sackville, flax had been grown and linen woven in the latter part of the nineteenth century. Westmorland County, however, is primarily Acadian French and this, combined with distance and the passage of time, proved to be an effective screen. Nell knew nothing of the development. Closer in time, in 1919, Marie Louise Blanchard of Caraquet, in the northeast of the province, opened a workshop in which she and fellow workers made carpets from linen and wool produced in the district. But Caraquet was a world away from St. Andrews, and possibly from Ottawa too. Mme Blanchard was not only a contemporary of Nell's (she was born in 1871) but a kindred spirit, who from her shop in Caraquet, sold beautifully woven linens. Like Nell, she liked to proselytize, giving talks in schools and convents and to groups of interested adults. She encouraged young and old to value tradition and to embrace a liberal education. She also planted her own flax in the spring and harvested and processed it in the fall.

Fibre flax seed for an experimental planting was probably sent to Nell by the Department of Agriculture in time for the 1918 growing season, but in that year and the one following, she was unable to organize the test. She wrote to the department again in January 1920 to ask whether two-year-old seed would still be viable and to request more information on methods of flax fibre production. It is unclear how the project stood when Nell went to England later that year but it is tempting to speculate that while there she discussed the idea in the household of another of her second cousins who had roots in St. Andrews.

Florence Moody, a sister of Dr. Neville Parker, was the wife of Harry Moody who until he retired in 1905, was the London secretary of the CPR. In that capacity he would have been thoroughly familiar with the work of the railway's Department of Colonization and Development. This department took an active role in promoting agricultural and industrial enterprise, working in tandem with the Dominion government, to provide economic opportunities for the immigrants brought from Britain by the CPR on its steamships and moved across Canada on its rails. Harry Moody may well have suggested to Nell that the Department of Colonization and Development might help her with her linen project and that she should make contact through the CPR people who summered regularly in St. Andrews. In any case, by the summer of 1922, Colonel J.S. Dennis, chief commissioner of the Department of Colonization and Development, and Major G.G. Ommanney, its development engineer, were replying to letters written on Nell's behalf by C.R. Hosmer and Sir Thomas Tait. Charles Hosmer and Thomas Tait, longtime summer residents of St. Andrews, were retired CPR executives who continued to wield influence and they obligingly helped Nell to pull strings. On October 9, Colonel Dennis assured Mr. Hosmer, "We have been having considerable correspondence with Miss Mowat regarding this matter, and are, of course, anxious to do everything we can to help her." He went on to explain that his department considered the production of fibre flax extremely important, that it had conducted extensive experiments over the preceding three years and brought an expert from Belgium to supervise the work, and that they now had produced high quality seed and fibre. They hoped Canada would soon take the place of Russia which had produced 80 percent of the world's flax fibre before the 1914-18 war, and then its own political revolution in 1917. Nell wasn't thinking in quite such ambitious terms. A successful cash crop would be an obvious benefit to Charlotte County farmers but initially, at least, she simply wanted to produce linen fabric for craft work on the same basis as wool homespun.

Major Ommanney, the development engineer, became her main contact. Despite thinking in larger terms than Nell, he was very helpful in the following six years, supplying advice and facts and figures about fibre production, and eventually assisting her with two other projects as well. To begin with, he sent her on October 27, 1922, a bag of 225 pounds of the special flax seed developed by his department, free of charge. While she travelled around Charlotte County planning the winter's work with the crafters, Nell talked up the linen project and enlisted eighteen farmers who would each plant either an acre or a half acre of flax in the summer of 1923.

By that time, the pottery was on the brink of becoming a reality. Bernard Kane had made successful pots with the Charlotte County clay samples and promptly sent the test pieces to her, as well as a plan for a simple building that would house a pottery. He was agreeing to come and help her. On December 13, 1920, she wrote expressing her delight with both the pots and Bernard's willingness, and suggested business terms for their joint enterprise in St. Andrews. She confidently proposed forming "a small company, say ten men who would put in one thousand dollars each that might give us enough to start on, then we could promise you a salary of $2,000 until the thing began to pay expenses, after that you could demand a percentage of the earnings before we declared dividends. I think I would do the same myself. What percentage would you be willing to consider?" Nell also told Bernard that she had just been talking over the pottery idea with friends from Montreal in whose opinions she had confidence.

They were very enthusiastic and suggested that she go to Montreal after Christmas "to meet a wealthy Canadian there who is interested in developing the resources of Canada." The friends from Montreal were Hayter and Kate Reed, newly retired from their respective careers as manager-in-chief and chief decorator of all the CPR hotels. Experienced, powerful, and sympathetic friends, indeed. Things were looking auspicious and Nell encouraged Bernard to think of coming overseas the following April, pending only the outcome of her efforts to raise capital. In the meantime, she would assemble a list of available town properties where the pottery could be built. "I hope you will like St. Andrews," she wrote. "The scenery is very beautiful, all hills and sea and islands. In summer, it is gay with tourists. In winter, there is very little going on, that is why I am so anxious to start a pottery as there are so few industries and so little for the young people to go in for, so the best of them all leave the place as soon as they grow up. I think there will be no difficulty in finding workers."

During the next twelve months, Nell needed all her optimism and determination. When she went to Montreal in February, the Reeds' wealthy friend apparently declined the invitation to invest, but a handful of other businessmen helped her fashion a prospectus and promised to buy shares in the proposed company. While there, she also had an opportunity to show Bernard's samples to a firm of wholesale china dealers, Cassidy & Company, in the hope of finding a single source of capital and thus obviating the need to form a company. Great enthusiasm on the part of Cassidy's chief buyer fizzled into cautious indecision, however, in the hands of their Saint John agent. By early April, Nell, chafing at the delay, pressed on and recruited five St. Andrews businessmen who agreed to form a company with her and buy $100 shares. Nell's aim now was to raise $15,000 immediately by selling a total of 150 shares. This, however, meant applying for a charter from the provincial government, entailing another delay of several weeks. No share moneys could be collected until the creation of a legal entity. Nell's own money at this time of year was entirely invested in stock for the approaching summer season.

When she wrote to Bernard Kane in late April 1921, she had promises for $5,000 and hoped the project would be well enough in hand for him and his family to come from England during the summer. This would still allow time for him to supervise construction of the pottery building and the kiln, and produce some saleable goods "in time to catch the Christmas trade." Their steady correspondence throughout these months dealt with many questions provoked by this new and specialized enterprise: the availability and relative merits of British and Canadian fire brick for the proposed kiln, the fuel that should be used to fire the kiln, the availability of a local mason to build it, the import duties that would be levied on other pottery-making equipment, the lines of pottery that would probably sell best. As for a location for the kiln and pottery, one possibility was an old tannery on the waterfront that had closed several years earlier and was now used by fishermen for storing nets and gear. It was in a "frightful mess" but there is, she added, "a fascination to me always about utilizing waste material and bringing order out of chaos." Coal and possibly clay could be shipped by scow. Nell also wondered about cold weather, with which Bernard was unaccustomed, affecting the firing of the clay. She raised the question of whether to begin firing in the fall or wait until the following spring. There was also the question of living accommodations for the Kanes and, a concern of Mrs. Kane's, schools for their two younger children. Nell assured her of the adequacy of the town's schools — she herself was a product of them — and stressed the point, that may well have registered with the Kanes whose means were limited, that schools in Canada were "casteless." Offspring of the rich and the poor attended the same establishments.

Nell researched diligently and reported her findings on all these questions in letters to Bernard Kane that sometimes ran to six pages in length. But by mid-July 1921, she had to confess, "I have been through many discouraging places but have never once thought of abandoning the project." The problem was still the money:

To begin with Mr. Waycott (the man of whom I wrote

last who had left St. Andrews in his youth and returned
a millionair[e] prepared to take an interest in the town)
was very disappointing...I could not make him see the
artistic value of anything...he could not come down
to the idea of a small enterprise...used to dealing with
millions and large profits. He also said that this was
the worst year that had ever been known to finance an
enterprise like that. He said that money was all tied up
in the States...even people who had it could not get
at it — nothing was paying dividends...large manufacturing plants were running on half time or closing
down...business was stagnant.

Mr. Waycott had in fact given Nell a capsule description, confirmed
by other businesspeople she consulted, of a short economic depression that peaked that summer leaving three-and-a-half million people
unemployed in the United States and two-and-a-half million in
Britain. Undaunted, Nell claimed that "now was the time if ever to
make a pottery succeed." The china-store owners in town told her
that they could get very little stock from their usual British sources;
winter was coming on and people would need work more than ever,
so labour would be cheaper; and prosperity would have returned by
the time the pottery was established. But concern for the Kanes, who
were now hovering on the point of emigrating, weighed on her: "All
the time I worried that I had nothing definite to write to you. I knew
there was an alternative somewhere but for a while I could not see it,
now I know. I mean to tackle it alone if you will help me!"

Nell then outlined a new plan for a small start that could be
managed using $5,000 in bonds that she would cash in — her last
nest egg. In addition, she would provide a half acre of land behind
Chestnut Hall for the building of a kiln; the basement of Chestnut
Hall for a workshop; the services of two capable workmen already
on her payroll as assistants when needed; the services of a secretary;
accommodation for the Kanes in Chestnut Hall at a very favourable
rent; and a guaranteed salary of $2,000 for one year. "If at the end of

that time my money is gone and I see only dismal failure ahead (this I hardly think will be)," she wrote to him, "I will ask you to make your home with me until such time as you can find another berth." She concluded by asking Bernard to name his conditions, agreeing to sign a legal agreement between them, and leaving the exact date of his coming to Canada to his judgement. A week later, after a talk with an old and trusted lawyer friend, she wrote again offering "in addition to your salary of $2,000 per year, one third of the profits of the enterprise." She further proposed that "I keep one third myself and that one third be put into the business to purchase such improvements as we require until the plant is fully equipped. The management I shall want to place entirely in your hands, reserving only the designing for myself and the training of young people in rapid brush work and original designing, so that the work will always have that native element I have found so successful in my embroidery."

By September, negotiations for an equal partnership rather than a company began to cross the Atlantic in both directions, along with continuing discussion of the kiln fuel question. The Kanes decided to sail the next spring, in 1922. All the while, Bernard Kane was shipping over sample pieces made up from various clays and designs Nell sent him. These usually sold immediately in the shop but she kept some for display in the Cottage Craft booth at the St. Stephen Exhibition, promising would-be buyers that next year there would be pottery "from our own kiln" for sale. And, she reported having got a bargain in bricks. A mason had advised her to buy the bricks left over from the building of the new Bank of Nova Scotia, only two blocks away — of "excellent quality and going cheap" — for which she paid $150. In October Nell drove to Fredericton for a consultation with Dr. L.W. Bailey, a renowned professor of chemistry and natural sciences. He gave her further encouragement, along with a list of New Brunswick minerals that might prove useful for pottery glazes. Nell also received two boxes of labelled rock samples which she forwarded immediately to Bernard. She wrote that she "would like to find something that would provide us with pigment for colouring some unusual shade...I thought that green rock might do something but it burned out dull red." A year later, in November 1921, she received a sample of clay from a Mr. Robinson of Hillsboro, in Albert County, that she was told was self glazing when exposed to great heat and turned an unusual colour. There was no evidence that the clay had ever been worked (although it might have been tested) but the donor, nevertheless, was anxious to know what results Bernard could get with it. He was so anxious to establish industry in the province that he offered to ship a consignment of clay to St. Andrews at his own expense and if it proved satisfactory, to help finance a branch plant for utility ware in Albert County. Such questions could wait, but Nell relayed them to Bernard to reassure him that "the wilderness to which you are now coming has possibilities."

Fuel was the other major concern. Nell consulted with her cousin Captain Harry Mowat, formerly of Liverpool, England, where he was at one time commander of the fleet of CPR steamers. He had made an extensive investigation of the use of crude oil as fuel and, Nell wrote, "strongly advises us to use it for our kiln." The notes Captain Mowat made for Nell that were sent on by her to Bernard, are a model of logic, clarity, and detail. After listing, in his beautiful handwriting, the virtues of easy handling, even and constant temperature, intense heat, lack of dust and ash, he concluded, "I think owing to the size of the Kiln the most suitable oil would be from 860 to 910 spc Gravity which is more readily broken up through heat and sprayer into gas than heavier grades." Such an authoritative recommendation must have appealed to Nell who had considered several possible sources of fuel, including coal, by the schooner load, from Cape Breton, and locally cut wood. (Nell would buy the "stumpage" and hire a man to do the cutting; "any man in Canada," she wrote to Kane, " knows how to handle an axe.") Wood, however, was expensive, making oil, in Nell's eyes, a wonderful solution. Bernard promised to think about oil. If they decided on coal, Nell thought it might be mixed with the bark peeled off pulp logs. (Bark intensifies the heat of coal and could be bought for almost nothing.)

The terms of the equal partnership, which Bernard Kane wanted as some assurance of security for himself and his family, were agreed upon by late November. Each partner would provide $2,500 of capital, but Bernard's actual cash outlay would be $1,750, the other $750 of his share being accounted for by his expenses in moving across the Atlantic, loss of salary while in transit, and conversion of his sterling assets into Canadian dollars. Nell had legal documents drawn up by her lawyer in St. Stephen and sent them to Bernard for his signature with a few details left "still in pencil subject to your approval...there might be things which your business experience would prompt you to improve upon. I therefore leave it to you to trace in ink as you see fit those items I have left in pencil." The Kanes proceeded with the sale of their house, began to send boxes of their belongings to St. Andrews, and booked their passage on the ship *Corsican*, sailing to Saint John in mid-April 1922.

Nell was fully aware of her responsibility toward the Kanes and told them so in the letters she wrote to them in the six months before they left England. "I feel grateful to you for your courage and confidence in the enterprise and for giving up so much for an uncertainty," she wrote on November 29, 1921. "In all our dealings in the future I hope I may never forget this and I promise to do all I can to make up to you in Canada for the English home you have left behind." This endearingly forthright promise was served up on a platter garnished with paeans on the landscape of her own beloved Charlotte County. At the same time, however, she was conscious of the need to prepare the Kanes for the roughness and remoteness of the county compared to any place they would have known. The phrase "forest primeval" occurs several times but always in a positive context: "You see my beloved Province is about as large as England and only inhabited round the edges and along the rivers, and at the heart of it there are still forests primeval." Her sheer enthusiasm bursts through: "Do you know I believe we are a pioneer enterprise as there is no pottery in Canada that does artistic or ornamental ware, what few there are make only a cheap grade of cooking utensils from stock patterns that come from England. Surely we must succeed!"

By the close of 1921 Nell could report another successful year for Cottage Craft, despite the generally hard times. She told Gertrude

Pringle of *Maclean's*, one of the many journalists who visited St. Andrews in the twenties, that she had paid out more than $12,000 to her workers (crafters and local staff) and over $1,400 on materials (wool fleeces, dye, soap, and fabric for lining embroidered bags). The business had enjoyed an unusually busy Christmas season. It is likely that she was able to set aside from the shop receipts her entire $2,500 share of the pottery capital. Her $5,000 in bonds could remain uncashed and would serve as a safety net for the pottery. In addition, she had started a class "for the purpose of training the young people in painting and brush work so that if we need talent of that kind we will know where to find it."

The Kanes arrived during the third week of April 1922, nineteen months after the idea of their emigrating had first been raised and a whole year longer than Nell had hoped initially. Their vessel, the CPR's *Corsican*, was probably the last ship to dock at Saint John Harbour before ice closed the St. Lawrence River again the following winter. Nell wrote to Mrs. Kane telling her that she fully expected to meet the boat, adding modestly, that in case Mrs. Kane had forgotten what she looked like, she would be wearing a blue suit ("rather brightish blue") and brown furs. If Nell was unable to get there, the Kanes were to go to the Royal Hotel and have their bags sent to the CPR station. With Nell, or on their own (the *St. Croix Courier* did not specify), the Kanes arrived at St. Andrews on April 27. In her letters up to the time of their sailing, Nell had reiterated the apprehensions that were a leitmotif in her previous correspondence. To Mrs. Kane in March, she expressed admiration for her "courage in coming to this strange country with nothing here but the clay in the harbour." To Bernard Kane, in February, she wished that he could arrive in a "less forlorn" season, the bleakest of the year. With no new growth to lighten the dark rocks or soften the severe outlines of the black spruce, April in southwest New Brunswick could be a particularly cruel month. A countryside less like south Devon would be difficult to imagine. The land, too, she warned, might not have recovered "from its bondage of snow." But every apprehension was countered by an expression of her own love for her "wild rocky country" and "its simple kindly people" and the hope that the Kanes in time would come to share this love.

For their part, the Kanes, one suspects, were worried less about landscape and climate than about their economic prospects. In a letter to Nell just before he sailed, Bernard inquired about the prospects for opening an agency, presumably for an English pottery or potteries. Nell advised against it, asserting that St. Andrews was too far from the larger centres to make that kind of venture practical. But if he thought it feasible after he had seen the conditions, she would not stand in his way.

In town, the mood was expectant rather than apprehensive. In a long letter to the editor of the *Courier*, Robert Armstrong, former editor of the *Beacon*, wrote of Nell "blazing a new trail" by establishing the first plant for the manufacture of ornamental pottery in the Dominion. Bernard Kane, with his long experience of making ornamental ware for the English tourist trade, he considered the ideal man for the job. So great was the anticipation surrounding the pottery that Armstrong thought that it might even have a domino effect, reviving the defunct brick making industry. Once the Kanes had arrived, Nell's confidence rose. In an address in May to the Saint John branch of the Women's Canadian Club, she asserted that all the ingredients for a successful pottery were now in place: an expert English potter; local clays, which he had found to be eminently suitable; and local painters, whom she had begun training to decorate the pots.

Disappointments

The Kanes settled quickly into the social and cultural life of the town. In its social notes for June 15, the *Courier* reported that Mrs. Kane, assisted in serving by Miss Bessie Grimmer, received for the first time in the family quarters at Chestnut Hall. On July 6, she entertained a group of young people for her nine-year-old daughter Betty. In November, "little Miss Betty Kane," who like both her parents, was musical, played a piano solo at a Canadian authors evening hosted by the Women's Canadian Club. Bernard Kane also took to the stage. In December, he appeared in two tableaux ("Cotter's Saturday Night" and "We'd Better Bide a Wee"), another production of the Women's Canadian Club. And on Christmas Eve, he led a carolling group, which sang before the houses of shut-ins. At the St. Stephen Exhibition in September, he had also won first prize in the watercolour landscape painting division.

The Kanes' community activities, as reported in the local social pages, continued throughout the winter and spring of 1923. Mrs. Kane entertained the monthly evening bridge club from January until May, and in late February, she organized a children's concert for fifty guests. In March, she was hostess to the St. Andrews Church Guild. In late May, Bernard Kane, accompanied by Mrs. Kane, sang a solo during the interval at the most prestigious cultural event of that year:

an address by Bliss Carman, followed by readings of his poems, held under the auspices of the Women's Canadian Club. That same week Mrs. Kane held a musical afternoon for pupils and parents.

There was also steady progress at the pottery. While no details of the construction of a kiln remain, one was built, presumably under Kane's supervision, behind Chestnut Hall. Kane also organized a pottery class, teaching his charges how to mould pottery and, more difficult, how to throw it on the potter's wheel. In what might have been interpreted as a show of independence, he also demonstrated how to decorate small objects for the tourist trade. The pottery, made from good quality clay from the head of tide in the Digdeguash, was an attractive red colour. After moulding or throwing, the pots were dipped in white slip glaze and then fired. Coloured designs were painted on the white background and the pots were fired again. To reveal the underlying red clay, designs were sometimes inscribed through the wet slip before the first firing. According to Nell's protégé and longtime employee Frances Wren, Mr. Kane and his sons did most of the work. (Frances Wren, who went on to teach arts and crafts, including painting and drawing, at Macdonald College in Montreal, began working for Cottage Craft in her high school years. After school and during the summers she worked in the pottery and helped in the shop.) On December 7, 1922, the *Courier* reported that these days in St. Andrews all eyes were on the pottery. In what may have been its first commercial operation, the kiln was about to be fired again to fix the glaze on the baked or finished pots. The opening of the kiln, the *Courier* noted, was "eagerly looked forward to."

The first and only public hint of discord came in the form of a *Courier* social note on May 17, 1923. It read simply: "Bernard Kane has returned from Montreal, Toronto and Medicine Hat." In Toronto and Montreal he might have been investigating potential markets, but Medicine Hat, the home of the renowned Medalta stoneware pottery, offered no such prospects. The Medalta pottery specialized in functional kitchenware: Brown Betty teapots and earthenware containers. On September 13, the cryptic May notice was followed by another, equally brief but unambiguous: "Mr. and Mrs. Kane, Lawrence and

Betty Kane, left Monday for East Liverpool, Ohio, where they expect to make their home." East Liverpool, in the Ohio valley, was America's "Crockery City."

What went wrong? How could so careful, open-hearted and promising a prelude have ended so abruptly? Bernard Kane may have quickly concluded that the scale of the pottery operation in St. Andrews was too small and the market too limited to satisfy him. The "agency" that he had in mind before coming was, as Nell had warned, a risk in remote St. Andrews. But the suddenness of their departure after Nell's repeated assurances that she would carry them for at least a couple of years, and the breadth

Bernard Kane, on right, and the pottery kiln at Chestnut Hall.
Courtesy of the Charlotte County Archives

of the Kanes' social commitments, suggests deeper discontents. The only surviving clue is a reference to the Kanes in a letter to Nell from her young friend Kim Osburn, daughter of Henry Osburn, the St. Andrews manager of the New Brunswick and Canada Railway, dated July 29, 1923. "I did hear," she wrote, "that the Kanes had folded their tents like Arabs — leaving [young] Bernie behind with you. Things always work out about as you want them to." Her colourful but possibly misleading opening phrase hints at a swift departure from Chestnut Hall, if not from the town. Less open to interpretation is the sentence that follows: Nell, it would seem, had wished, possibly even willed, their departure. If so, what prompted it? Nell was by now a celebrity, courted by clubs and the press, and she simply may have been jealous. The talented Kanes bounded onto the St. Andrews stage like seasoned troupers, possibly offending her *amour-propre* by diverting attention away from her. The more likely explanation, however, is that the Kanes threatened not so much Nell's self-esteem but the integrity of her creation, Cottage Craft. Her mantra, repeated over and over, was that all Cottage Craft products should reflect the life and landscape of Charlotte County — "tell the story of our life here." Early in her negotiations with Bernard, she had insisted that she would train talented young people to do the decorative work. "The management," she wrote in July 1921, "I shall want to place entirely in your hands, reserving only the designing for myself and the training of young people." She repeated her intention the following December, three months before the Kanes sailed: "I have started a class for the purpose of training the young people in painting and brush work." That Nell meant what she said about controlling design was evident from her reaction to a set of decorated cups Kane sent from England in December 1920. Nell praised the cups but added a rider that she thought she could make an "easier design." For an outgoing man of obvious flair and talent, the role of production manager of a small pottery in a small, isolated town could not have satisfied for long. As a functionary making, as opposed to designing and decorating, pots, he would fare better in Medicine Hat or East Liverpool. In other words, he may not have sat well under Nell's philosophical umbrella and, with a new world beckoning, may have decided to try his luck elsewhere.

However disruptive Kane's departure might have been, it did not bring down the pottery. His elder son Bernie, who at the time was courting the bank manager's daughter, stayed on to manage it. Frances Wren described him as "very skillful," but after a year he also left, signing on with a company that owned ocean-going oil tankers. The work of the pottery was carried on by three of the "apprentices," one of whom was the gifted Frances Wren. The other two, both boys, prepared the clay, made the pottery, and fired it, while Frances applied the decoration. The wood-burning kiln took two-and-a-half days to fire a thousand pieces. Finally, one winter, frost cracked the chimney from top to bottom. It was the end of pottery making at Chestnut Hall, but a few years later, Nell, using an oil-fired kiln, opened a new, smaller pottery on the waterfront at Pagan Street. Her choice of quarters was the same disused tannery she had mentioned to Bernard Kane. The combination of old, weathered wood and fuel oil proved too great a temptation to fire and within a few years, the building burned. According to Frances Wren, that was the end of pottery making in St. Andrews. However, the *Courier* for April 6, 1939 reported the building of a small showroom to display pottery in the ell of the Ocean Products building, a business established in 1938 to produce rockweed meal. Most of the pieces were made from moulds but some were thrown on a potter's wheel. The designs were glimpses of the harbour, old wharves, buildings, boats, and weirs, as seen from the workroom window. From a mould made by Nell, medallions of the King and Queen were being prepared to coincide with the royal visit in 1939. The clay used, reportedly, was much superior to the local clay formerly used, and consequently the wares were of much finer quality. Miss Mowat, "the owner and soul of this little industry," was recorded as saying that she would be content if the pottery could be made to pay its way without profit. Edna Higgins, who worked at the pottery for two summers in the late thirties, confirms the *Courier*'s report. All the pieces were made from moulds and the decoration was of the simplest kind: "Miss Mowat would come in and show us what she wanted, for instance a very simple ashtray, she would take it and do the edge like you do a pie and then add a crow or a sheep on the side. We would be doing only very simple things." It was a far cry from Bovey Tracey, Bernard Kane, and the heady visions of the 1920s.

Nell's flax and linen project ended just as disappointingly as the pottery. In their exchanges with Nell, Charles Hosmer, Sir Thomas Tait, Colonel J.S. Dennis, and Major G.G. Ommanney were invariably courteous and encouraging. Although retired, Mr. Hosmer and Sir

Thomas Tait were still powerful men and almost certainly would have held large blocks of CPR shares. As senior officers of the company, Colonel Dennis and Major Ommanney were obliged to to encourage farm and related industrial production in all parts of the Dominion within reach of its lines. From the outset, however, a fundamental, and ultimately unbridgeable, divide existed between the CPR's interests and Nell's. While eager to encourage local enterprise, the CPR, as a mighty corporation, was chiefly interested in large-scale developments that would create business for the company and attract farming settlement to its unoccupied lands. Were Canada to become a major producer of flax, the CPR would be the chief carrier of seed and baled flax fibre. Nell on the other hand, was interested only in sufficient yields of flax to supply her cottage industry and provide a cash crop for "her people" — marginal Charlotte County farmers. Both Colonel Dennis and Major Ommanney also would have known that rockbound Charlotte County was the least fertile county in a province that, with the exception of its two main river valleys, was hardly renowned for its agriculture.

The language of their exchange is instructive. Major Ommanney and Colonel Dennis allude repeatedly to the small scale of Nell's proposed operation. In his reply to C.R. Hosmer, J.S. Dennis acknowledged the receipt of a letter about the cultivation of flax "in a small way," noting later that flax production could be of such importance to Canada that he and his staff had been urging farmers to take it up "in a large way." To emphasize the point, he observed that the department for the previous three years had conducted extensive experiments with seed imported from Ireland, both in southern Ontario and on irrigated lands in Alberta, and had brought out an expert from Belgium to supervise the work. In spite of his reservations, Colonel Dennis offered to provide seed for experimental plots, free transport for an adviser, and free transport of the flax to a processing mill, provided these expenses could be charged to the CPR's flax experiment budget. In a letter to Nell, Charles Hosmer repeated the phrase "in a small way" and, with his own reputation to protect, asked her "to think the matter over carefully and see if it is worthwhile."

G.G. Ommanney, Nell's chief contact at the CPR, agreed that flax could be grown successfully in the Maritime Provinces but he felt that a commercial flax fibre industry could be conducted on "primitive lines." Labour costs in Canada were higher than in Europe, obliging Canadian growers to adopt scientific methods and labour-saving devices. He advised her to think in larger terms, of the organization of a company and the building of a modern processing mill, which by converting the raw flax into fibre, would more or less assure the farmers of a market. He surmised, incorrectly, that her intention was merely to "encourage" the farmers, and that the "commercial end "of the enterprise did not appeal to her. Nell may not have been a bookkeeper but she was a businesswoman who understood fully the need for profit.

In the same letter G.G. Ommanney referred to Oswald Cattley, an expert in the flax fibre industry, who had called on him in Montreal and who, probably at his suggestion, had visited the Cottage Craft stand at the Canadian National Exhibition in Toronto in late August or early September, 1922. Oswald Cattley, who was then seventy-two, came from a family of flax brokers who formed part of an English colony in St. Petersburg, Russia. He had been a merchant as well as a mine manager and engineer in Russia, Siberia, and the Caucasus. He was also a fellow of the Royal Geographical Society and, in a family history, is described as a Siberian explorer. He retired to England, presumably after the Great War and the collapse of the Russian economy. He was paying a visit to his son at Ogdensburg, New York, and sick of his role as a "drone in the human hive," looking for occupation. When, in September 1922, Nell wrote to him asking if he would come to St. Andrews to advise her farmers, he agreed readily and graciously. As he was short of funds at the time, he thought it best if he attended the harvesting at the end of the next growing season. Aside from weeding, flax needed little attention until ready to be harvested. He also offered to help with marketing if, in due course, she needed it. Advised by Nell that each farmer would be issued with a pound weight of flax seed, he suggested sowing a patch six yards by six, "broadcast and pretty close." The ground should be prepared that fall and the seed bed made as clean as possible in the spring.

On learning that Nell intended to give only one pound of seed to each farmer, G.G. Ommanney, who was uncomfortable with anything done on a small scale, informed her that he would send a three-and-a-half bushel bag of seed, approximately two hundred pounds, that would be enough to sow two acres. He suggested experimental plots of one eighth of an acre, each sown with twelve pounds of seed. If, as Nell had indicated, she could distribute seed to 100 farmers then he would send six bags together with directions for soil preparation and sowing. The acreage sown, roughly twelve-and-a-half acres, should produce at least one hundred and twenty-five bushels of seed — enough to sow fifty acres the following season. If cultivation were concentrated fairly centrally around one point then it would justify the building of a small, hand-operated mill. He promised to get an estimate of costs from the Dominion government's Central Experimental Farm in Ottawa. Oswald Cattley, too, on discovering that Nell could get as much seed as she required, suggested larger experimental plots, of an acre or half acre.

In the fall of 1923, a field inspector, probably Mr. Deltour from the Dominion Department of Agriculture, examined the crop. The report, written on letterhead from the Kennedy Hotel in St. Andrews, is unsigned and undated. The inspector examined sixteen acres of flax grown by twenty different farmers. He found great quantities of weeds but in only two cases did weeds pose a serious difficulty in harvesting. In each of these cases, he was able to save the seed but the straw had to be destroyed. In the report, he also described how the flax should be harvested and processed. After pulling (cutting would reduce the length of the fibre), the straw should be tied in sheaves, stacked, and dried. To separate the fibres from the surrounding stalk, the flax had to be "retted" or rotted, either in standing or flowing water, or spread out to rot in the fields. Retting required many hands and had to be supervised by an experienced man or woman. Once free of the stalk, the fibres were separated from the woody inner core by a breaking machine and then, if of good quality, separated into strands ("scutched") for the making of linen thread. Otherwise, the fibres were bundled and sold as "toss flax," or tow, to the upholstery trade. The author of the report recommended that the current crop be converted into upholsterers' tow and an effort be made to sell it in Montreal.

In addition to supplying seed for the experimental plots, the obliging G.G. Ommanney contacted R. J. Hutchinson, chief of the Division of Economic Fibre Production of the Department of Agriculture, who agreed, in a letter forwarded to Nell, to process 100 pounds of flax straw that she could send to the Central Experimental Farm. The straw would be retted and scutched and if the fibre was of the required standard he would offer advice about the installation of a mill. In his accompanying letter on October 23, 1923, Major Ommanney, who was still uneasy about the scale of the Charlotte County operation, appended the rider: "BIG WLD BE BETTER — GET LGE SHARE OF MARKET." In a letter a month later, realizing that Charlotte County farmers could never be major producers of flax, he advocated that she scale down, producing only enough for locally made linen fabric for the tourist market. He understood that there was an Irish farmer near St. Andrews with some experience of "the flax game" and wondered if he might be able to make the required machinery from inexpensive material. The growers would need a small mill with a whipping plant for deseeding; a fanning and cleaning mill for cleaning the seed; a couple of breakers for breaking the straw; and perhaps five scutching knives for separating the fibre. Hutchinson, he reported, estimated that second-hand machinery might be bought for around $500. To avoid the cost of spinning and weaving machines, local women might be induced to spin and weave by the old hand methods during the winters.

Admitting that he had done as much as he could officially, he suggested, strictly between themselves, that she might try to interest prominent summer residents in the enterprise, including the CPR's own chairman and president, "more or less as a hobby," letting them know of the Department of Development and Colonization's interest. In a subsequent letter, on December 18, 1923, he suggested that she might have more success approaching them in summer when they would be on holiday and likely in a "more genial mood...than in their offices." In the same letter, Major Ommanney informed her of the death of the courtly Oswald Cattley, "who might have been of great assistance in developing [the flax] industry in Canada." Possibly worn down by inactivity, Oswald Cattley had departed the human hive a year earlier, on December 22, 1922.

By the beginning of 1924, however, Nell had decided on a more formal, official approach to E.W. Beatty, the president of the CPR. She informed G.G. Ommanney of her decision, and in a letter, dated February 21. Major Ommanney, after a consultation with J.S Dennis, made several suggestions. First, she should explain that what she had in mind was a "homestead flax industry," based on approximately 100 acres of fibre flax that would be processed locally by a small mill. (The mill and machinery would cost about $5,000.) Second, she should refer to the help already given by their own department and mention that the Central Experimental Farm in Ottawa had been very satisfied with the quality of flax grown by Charlotte County farmers. She should also emphasize that a local cottage industry would give occupation to farmers' wives, as well as to farmers, and that the extra farm income might induce young people to stay in their own country, instead of migrating to the New England States. Lastly, in what can only be regarded as his lack of confidence in the success of the application, he suggested that in view of the CPR's large interest in St. Andrews, she encourage CPR executives to invest in the project.

Nell's last serious fling of the dice in the direction of the CPR failed, as G.G. Ommanney had feared. She continued to write to him on other matters, but there is a long break in the flax correspondence. In 1927, when it resumes, Nell had turned her attention to the Dominion Department of Agriculture. On April 11, 1927 she received a letter from E.S. Archibald, director of the Central Experimental Farm, written in response to appeals for government assistance. Not satisfied with the result of the 1923 experiment, Mr. Archibald suggested that five Charlotte County farmers be directed to plant a one-quarter-acre plot with government-supplied seed. This, he asserted, should provide "authentic information" as to the quality and yield of Charlotte County flax. Moreover, R.J. Hutchinson,

Dear Mr Kane

As it will be only about a month till you are here I am going to send you a few directions about your arrival. I fully expect to be in St. John to meet you and hope to be at the boat landing when you arrive. You may have forgotten what I look like but I will wear a blue suit (rather brightish blue) and brown furs so you can recognize me more easily. I think I will know you when I see you. If [for] any reason I am not [able] go to the ... there ... in St. John. Royal ...

in St. John.

I am so anxious to have you come and to have things really started. I admire your courage in coming to this strange country with nothing here but the clay in the harbour. I sincerely hope that neither you or Mrs Kane will ever regret this step.

I hope you will have a safe and pleasant voyage and enjoy the rest and change of life at sea which I am sure you both need.

Your boxes have not come yet but I have spoken of them at the custom house and they will keep them safely there till you arrive and can enter them yourself.

I hope you will learn to care for this land as much as I do.

Ever very sincerely yours
N. Helen Mowat-

Letter from Nell to Bernard Kane. Courtesy of the Charlotte County Archives chief of the Division of Economic Fibre Production, would come down from Ottawa to instruct the farmers in methods of harvesting. (R.J.Hutchinson, a northern Irishman, was an expert in flax fibre production who had learned his trade in Armagh, Stuttgart, and Bruges.) The flax fibre produced would be processed in a scutching mill at the Department of Agriculture's Fredericton Experimental Station.

The experiment, however, was not as conclusive as hoped. There is no evidence that Mr. Hutchinson ever inspected that particular harvest, but the flax was taken to Fredericton. In a report dated November 30, 1927, C. B. Bailey, head of the Fredericton Experimental Station, reported wide variations in yields which he attributed to differences in the preparation of the plots and to variations in their size; they had not been measured accurately. The flax, however, appeared to have been of good quality though much of it, due to continuously wet weather that made it difficult to get the plants under cover, had been "over retted," causing the fibres to break. As a result, they were not of linen quality and would have to be sold as "toss flax" or upholsterer's tow. The problem now was that there was not enough for a carload and manufacturers were interested only in carload lots.

Aside from the inexperience of the growers, the chief obstacle to progress in Charlotte County was the absence locally of a processing plant. R.J. Hutchinson, who had no obligations to the CPR or to St. Andrews, was unwilling to build one because of the small scale of the operation and continuing uncertainty as to the quality of the flax. He grudgingly conceded that he would consider providing a scutching machine if the CPR would cover the costs of a building and power, and enough farmers were willing to grow flax. His minimum requirement was twenty-five farmers, each committed to growing at least one acre. He also noted, pointedly, that in Nova Scotia the provincial government offered considerable help to farmers. Nell's response, written as a note on his letter but perhaps never conveyed, was that John Gidden, a feed and general merchant at Rollingdam, had offered the use of a building and a gasoline engine.

The following April, in 1928, J.H. Grisdale, the deputy minister of agriculture in Ottawa, reported to Norman Wilson, a former Liberal MP who summered near St. Andrews, that, in response to more badgering from the relentless Miss Mowat, three high-ranking officers of the CPR and the Dominion Department of Agriculture (Ommanney, Archibald, and Hutchinson) had met in Ottawa to consider the flax question in Charlotte County. In a note to "Helen," acknowledging her letter to him, Norman Wilson reported that he had read parts of her letter aloud to "the Doctor" (Grisdale) but, discretion overcoming valour, he had left out the part about "white collars." The result of this meeting was a decision to conduct yet another experiment but on a larger scale than in the previous year. G.G. Ommanney reported the gist of the discussion to Nell. Both Mr. Archibald and Mr. Hutchinson felt that it was a little too early to place a mill in Charlotte County, but he had been able to persuade them that there could be no resolution until they could get a reasonable acreage planted and the crop harvested and retted under proper supervision. Major Ommanney and the CPR would look after the growing of the flax and the shipping of the straw to the scutching mill at Fredericton, while the flax division of the Department of Agriculture would supervise the deseeding and retting. This, surely, as R.J. Hutchinson declared in a letter to Nell, on April 24, 1928, would determine whether flax growing in Charlotte County could be a commercial success.

R.J. Hutchinson's pointed reference to the Nova Scotia government's support of flax growing had been an unnecessary goad. While waiting for a decision from Ottawa, Nell had written to A. J. Murray, the New Brunswick superintendent of immigration and industry. She referred to a meeting with him and P.C. Armstrong of the CPR in the premier's office in Saint John more than a year previously. The farmers were interested, meetings were held, and an expert had been sent from Ottawa to explain the operation of a small flax mill. All were hopeful that by the following autumn, 1927, a flax industry would be well established in Charlotte County.

A week before writing to A.J. Murray, Nell also wrote to R.J. Hutchinson, wondering when they might expect seed. Instead of a confirmation of shipping came a bombshell: a memorandum from R.J. Hutchinson, dated April 7, 1928, entitled "Reasons for not Establishing Flax in Charlotte County." The objections ranged from the general (doubts about the suitability of the soil and the commercial viability of the enterprise) to the specific (no scutching mill and no promise of help from the CPR.) She enclosed a copy of the memo with her letter to Mr. Murray. For anyone less obdurate, a damning memo from the head of Canada's Department of Economic Fibre would have been a *coup de grâce*, but Nell was unbowed. She characterized Mr. Hutchinson's list as "Government Excuses" and insisted that it was essential a scutching unit be built that year because without one it would be impossible to sustain the interest of the farmers who were tired of experimenting. She implored Mr. Murray to do as much as he could and if necessary, to persuade the premier to exert his authority. By now practised in ways of applying pressure, she reminded him that flax mills had been built in Nova Scotia but none in New Brunswick. She also disclosed that she hadn't yet told the farmers of Ottawa's reluctance to provide a scutching machine, adding pointedly: "You know what it means when they get down on the Government." Nell was confident that he "would understand the situation." A.J. Murray evidently did. On April 30, 1928, he wrote to Nell disclosing that he had visited the Central Experimental Farm in Ottawa, talked to Mr. Hutchinson, and was satisfied that everything possible was being done.

In the meantime, Nell, ignoring R.J. Hutchinson's damning assessment, kept up her own attack on Ottawa. She wrote to E.S. Archibald, Hutchinson's superior officer, reiterating the importance of maintaining the farmers' interest. Despite many disappointments, they still hoped to have a flax mill established by the coming fall. John Gidden, who bought and sold feed, had a suitable building, and his place was very central. She reminded Mr. Archibald that the cool, humid atmosphere of the Bay of Fundy was very similar to Ireland's and that the farmers were anxious to work extensively. She also suggested that any further experimenting and processing be done in Charlotte County, not in Fredericton.

A week later, on May 2, she also wrote to Major Ommanney, thanking him for all his help and regretting the continual backsliding of the Dominion goverment. She asked one final favour: would he reverse a previous offer of taking two carloads of flax fibre to Fredericton and instead bring the little scutching mill from Fredericton to Charlotte County, the only significant producer of flax in the province. All the flax grown in the rest of the province, she added dismissively, could be sent by parcel post. (She repeated this same message to Mr. Archibald: Frederictonians didn't know how to run the mill and couldn't be bothered to learn.) She also suggested that he was too charitable to Mr. Archibald and the government in general. She and the farmers of Charlotte County had been on an eleven-year quest and at critical moments they had always been let down on the grounds that the Department of Agriculture could not tell definitely if the venture would pay. If they cannot do that, she exclaimed, what is the use of a Department of Agriculture?

Nell clearly still had some fight left in her, but there was, alas, no victory. In early May 1928, E.S. Archibald wrote that it would not be possible for anyone from Ottawa to visit Charlotte County for some little time. Mr. Hutchinson was on his way to Ireland, and it would be a while before Mr. Deltour, the field inspector, could pay a visit. Instead of a scutching machine, Mr. Hutchinson had arranged to send a breaking machine and promised to send Mr. Deltour to supervise the conversion of the crop into upholsterer's tow. In late November, Major Ommanney informed Nell that he had heard wind of a report of a good deal of flax straw, that had not been broken into tow, lying around in Charlotte County barns. So great were the difficulties of producing high-grade fibre in Canada that he feared the whole flax industry would develop along lines of producing a good grade of tow rather than fibre for linen. In March 1929, the implacable R.J. Hutchinson wrote Nell to ask if the farmers had been able to dispose of their green tow, and if she had plans for the coming season. But in April, he countered this concession by writing to say that he was mystified by failures of the breaking machine. The machine was simple to operate and the frequency of the breakdowns suggested to him that the farmers were not interested enough to operate it properly. Nell replied that he should not be surprised if the farmers were losing interest; they had had a great deal to discourage them. Even she, Nell ended, had been discouraged to the point of giving up. It was the end of the correspondence, and the end of the flax venture.

Watercolour by Nell of Charlotte County farmland. Courtesy of Aileen Smith

The shoreline of Passamaquoddy Bay, also by Nell. Courtesy of Sheila Simpson

Blankets and skeins of knitting yarn drying at Beech Hill, circa 1955.
Courtesy of Basil Lowery

A web of dyed homespun being stretched for drying
on wooden racks. Courtesy of Basil Lowery

Washed and dyed wool fleeces drying at Beech Hill.

Courtesy of Basil Lowery

Nell examining wool fleeces at Beech Hill, circa 1955.

Courtesy of Basil Lowery

Watercolour by Nell of a wharf and harbour at St. Andrews.

Courtesy of Andrew Leighton

Sketch by Nell for a hooked rug. Courtesy of the Charlotte County Archives

LILAC TIME.

MISS G. HELEN MOWAT. 1932.

"Miss Mowat on the Highway" by that Puckish, elfin
talent Frances Wren. Courtesy of the Charlotte County Archives

Wool collage of sailboat and bay by Nell.
Courtesy of Bunny Campbell

Wool collage of landscape with sheep.

Courtesy of the late E.B. and Elizabeth Ross

The Pansy Patch
by Frances Wren.

Courtesy of the Ross Memorial
Museum

Needlepoint of winter scene with fox.
Courtesy of the Ross Memorial Museum

"Bringing Home the Tree" by Helen Gilman.
Courtesy of the late E.B. and Elizabeth Ross

Framed needlepoints of winter and summer scenes by Helen Gilman.

Courtesy of the late E.B. and Elizabeth Ross

"Summer Courtship" and "Country Road" needlepoints.

Courtesy of the late E.B. and Elizabeth Ross

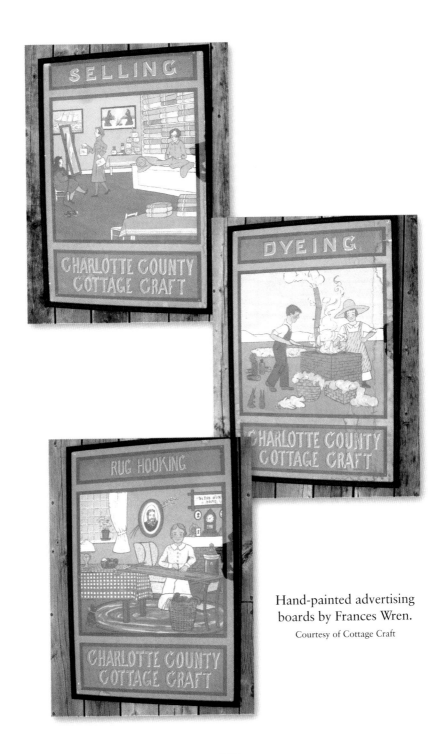

Hand-painted advertising boards by Frances Wren.

Courtesy of Cottage Craft

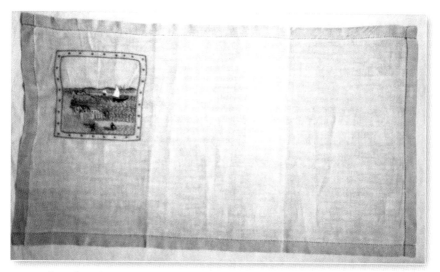

Embroidered napkin by Helen Gilman. Courtesy of the Ross Memorial Museum

Mug with cottage.

Courtesy of Cottage Craft

Mug with fenced landscape.

Courtesy of Cottage Craft

Assorted woven handbags.

Courtesy of Cottage Craft

Merry **C**hristmas

When Christmas Cards are out of fashion
And my ideas are on a ration.
When blackouts and the A.R.P.
Warn me of dangers yet to be
And headlines in the daily press
Constantly fill me with distress,
Yet still I feel in spite of these
I can rejoice in Christmas trees.
Therefore I send this card to say
Aren't you glad it's Christmas day?

Wartime
Christmas card
by Nell.

Courtesy of the Ross
Memorial Museum

Portrait by Nell of King George III,
done on wallpaper.

Courtesy of Andrew Leighton

Sketch by Nell of dancing at a Cottage Craft summer pageant.

Courtesy of the Ross Memorial Museum

"Merry Maritimers," a watercolour by Nell.

Courtesy of the Sir James Dunn Academy, St. Andrews

Portrait of Nell by Joyce McNichol.
Courtesy of Cottage Craft

Bowl with winter scene.
Courtesy of the late E.B. and
Elizabeth Ross

Cottage Craft dolls. Courtesy of Sheila Simpson

"John Passa" and "Marie Maquoddy." Courtesy of Sheila Simpson

Cottage Craft dolls and Frances Wren's map and whimsical
pictorial history of St. Andrews. Courtesy of the Charlotte County Archives

Float in town parade celebrating the seventy-fifth annniversary of
Cottage Craft, with Mary Janet Clift (knitting) and Nellie Crichton
(finishing a hooked rug). Courtesy of Mary Janet Clift

"A Factory of Twenty Square Miles"

Although Nell's pottery and flax ventures were disappointments, Cottage Craft continued to flourish in the 1920s. In the seven or eight years since its inception, local and regional newspapers had paid generous attention to the business. Summer visitors, too, had been invaluable emissaries, and from homes across the continent, they and their friends and neighbours placed orders for goods by mail. Sensing a market, large stores also sent for samples. So appealing were Cottage Craft products that by 1920 its embroidered homespun bags were being imitated by crafters working in the summer resort area known then as Murray Bay, now La Malbaie, on the north shore of the St. Lawrence, east of Quebec City. Descriptions of them as Murray Bay bags infuriated Nell. When questioned by journalist Ian Sclanders about the invention of the bags, she replied: "We made them fashionable and they were copied. When people go into a store to buy them now, they call them Murray Bay bags. Murray Bay bags indeed. When I hear them called that I always get as cross as a bull looking at a red flag. Because a little girl in Chamcook originated them."

By any business measure, Cottage Craft was a success, turning a profit and enjoying a reputation that was regional and, to some extent, national. Nell Mowat, as she remarked in one of her lectures, operated a "smokeless factory of twenty square miles" and employed more than 100 workers. Most small-business owners would have been content but for Nell, who had been schooled in the applied and decorative arts, commercial success alone was not enough. She wanted the recognition of her peers in the art world.

Each year, Charlotte County Cottage Craft had mounted displays of its goods at agricultural exhibitions in St. Stephen and Saint John. Then, around 1920 or 1921, Nell took the next logical step and entered a similar display in the Canadian National Exhibition in Toronto. Members of the Toronto branch of the Women's Art Association of Canada noticed the items on display, and in the fall of 1921, the group invited Cottage Craft to provide samples of needlework for the association's annual show in January 1922. The Toronto Women's Art Association was a catholic organization accommodating members who practised the fine arts of painting and sculpture, and provided they aspired to the ideals of the Arts and Crafts movement, the more workaday ones of weaving, knitting, and embroidery. Nell was delighted with the invitation, writing to the potter Bernard Kane: "We are very proud because the Toronto Art Association wants some of our work for their exhibition...This shows that we have the name of producing really artistic work." It was confirmation that Cottage Craft products had achieved that combination of beauty and utility to which all applied and decorative art aspires.

After an unusually brisk Christmas trade that year, which kept her "horribly busy," Nell assembled pieces of hand weaving, embroidery, and hooking and set off for Toronto on January 20. "I was glad to go," she later wrote Kane, "as it was almost the first recognition we have had from the artistic world, though commercially we have been successful. The exhibit was a success, several artists and other prominent people showing great interest and crediting Charlotte County with the development of a native Canadian Art." An enthusiastic report of the exhibit by a Toronto reporter was reprinted in the *St. Croix Courier* of February 2, 1922, but Nell's own description conveys the best sense of the occasion. Although this report to Kane was meant partly to reassure him that he would be joining a worthwhile enterprise, it also served Nell's storytelling instinct and her natural yen to share her own great pleasure in the significance of the entire event:

> The Toronto people made my visit there a very pleasant one but best of all was the coming home and telling my people how their work was received. In the heart of the country there is a little building known as the Foresters Hall. I hired this for the occasion and supplied abundance of hot coffee and asked everyone to bring sandwiches and cakes. It was a real party! They drove in wood sleds from miles around. The bottom of the sled filled with hay and patchwork quilts to wrap around them. There were about a hundred and twenty [people] altogether. After we had all the supper we wanted we went upstairs and they all sat down and listened to me while I told them of my Toronto adventures and how many people in Canada were looking to us as an example for creating native designs...[and that although] it almost seemed like a joke...it was not a joke and we had to work very hard and keep up a high standard and study nature very closely or we would lose the place we had gained...I reminded them of...their own pretty little homes among the fir trees on the hillsides and of the fields and apple orchards and lovely woodlands which were their very own and told them they had the best foundation for a Canadian National Art and if they very carefully represented these things in their rugs and embroideries they would surely succeed.

In October of that year she returned to the subject of the Toronto fair in an address to Cottage Craft workers in St. Andrews that was reported in the *Courier*:

> Wednesday afternoon a most delightful meeting of the Charlotte county cottage craft workers was held in the

parish hall. Miss G. Helen Mowat, in her usual bright and pleasing manner, welcomed the workers and said she hoped that these meetings would become semi-annual affairs. She then went on to speak about her exhibit at the Toronto exhibition and the amount of attention it had attracted. She spoke of the work of the cottage craft and how much it meant to the country to have an industry that would keep the young people at home instead of drifting to the States. She spoke of several ideas that might be worked out in connection with the cottage craft. A community produce store, a community dairy, a community woolen mill, and, above all, a flax industry. During the afternoon several charming choruses were sung by the Cottage Craft Choral Club. After the meeting delicious refreshments were served.

In many of Nell's references to the crafters as a group there was an unmistakably mother-hen tone. In her letter to Kane, she ended her description of the meeting at the Foresters Hall with, "I always feel great pride in my country people when I get them all together." Nell's possessiveness arose from a complex of social assumptions still prevalent at that period when people of even modest means usually had some daily paid, household help, and travel and education beyond the mid-secondary school level was available only to people who were relatively wealthy. Broadly speaking, Nell belonged to the class of educated employers, but in a town that was the seasonal home of some of the richest and most influential people on the continent, this was no guarantee of social position. She may have descended from a line of prominent Loyalists, and been able to claim a landowning or farming background, but she was now "in trade." As a self-made businesswoman she was helping to forge a meritocracy, an order based on achievement, not birth. As if to acknowledge this, there is no hint of condescension in her relationship with the individual crafters who worked alongside her, only of the respect for character and ability that she herself expected to meet in the world. Evidence of her quiet char-

Cottage Craft booth at the Saint John Exhibition, circa 1930.
Courtesy of the Ross Memorial Museum

ities toward workers in need is found in their letters of thanks to her; even then, the thanks are heartfelt but brief, and the writer usually goes on quickly to a subject of mutual interest. What comes through strongly in almost all the letters from crafters is genuine affection for Nell and appreciation for the new interest that the Cottage Craft connection has brought to their lives. The writer invariably closes with the hope that the household will very soon have the pleasure of a visit from her. She was a lively and forceful personality who enjoyed the company of her workers, and from her own experience, understood something of their often straitened circumstances and the demands of country life. "I expect you are very busy but I wish you had time to come up to see us," wrote Priscilla Lever from her farm home one day in early August 1923, when haying was in full swing and she herself had dressed over fifty chickens and fowl in the morning and could see she'd be feeding the haymakers late in the evening. She wrote the letter to send down to St. Andrews with a batch of embroidered bags that she and her mother had just completed. If there had been a contest to determine who was the most busy it would surely have been a draw.

One of the best examples of Nell's concern for the people of the county is the story she told Kane of a boy who came to the class she had set up to teach drawing and brush work to young people who might then work in the proposed pottery: "One little country lad started to walk fourteen miles to come and take a lesson. I am glad to say he got a chance to ride part of the way [it was December]." But a sobering sequel emerged at the party in the Foresters Hall two months later:

> I had a talk with...the boy I spoke to you of who walked so far to take a drawing lesson. He told me with deep disappointment that his father won't let him come any more. I offered to pay his fare on the train which brings him within four miles of his home but his father says art is all foolishness and there is no money in it. I consoled [the boy] by telling him that when the pottery started we would try and find a place for him there. I want to have a talk with the father, I don't know him at all, but there may be something to be said on his side, his wife died a year ago leaving him with four children...The old grandfather does the cooking for them and they have very little to live on. I dare say that in the crying needs of the present [the boy's] artistic dreams of the future irritate the poor man. I hope the pottery may give a happy solution to this problem, as it will to many others.

Another reason for the schoolmarmish tone that surfaced whenever Nell spoke to an assembly of crafters was that she was actually presenting a short course in art education and appreciation. She was teaching them to look at their own landscape with fresh, attentive eyes, as an artist would, and to find in it colours, lines, pictures, and patterns that they could transform into designs for textiles and, later, pottery. By insisting that no commercial patterns and borrowed designs be used she was forcing her workers-cum-students to discard visual clichés of all kinds and do the much harder work of looking and translating for themselves. This was a large undertaking for teacher and students alike, a difficult kind of re-education, and it was being attempted with a body of students scattered over a wide area. All the workers came together only once or twice a year, and for someone like Nell with a pedagogic bent, the opportunity for a lecture that reiterated the fundamental principles of their joint enterprise was irresistible. Anyone who wanted the Cottage Craft label on their handwork had to accept these basic conditions and most seemed willing to be taught. It would be surprising if there weren't some who took a "who does she think she is!" attitude, but those who signed on appreciated the enlargement of their lives, as well as the added income.

Nell's Christmas letters from her workers contained generous endorsements. In thanking Nell for her kindness and help, Amy Greenlaw of Leverville, whose husband Fred also helped with the weaving, confided that "without your work we would have to do without a good many things... Your coming into our home, has made it so different, and [hinting at some of the darker crosscurrents in country life] you can fully believe, we think just as much of you behind your back as we do to your face." Across the back of a large newborn lamb — an unusual arrival at that time of year — she wanted to write Cottage Craft in large letters. Amy's daughter Rhoda, to whom Nell sent a box of paints when she was sick, wrote to say that when Nell next came up "I will give you a great big kiss." She added a postscript: "Take care Miss Mowat don't get the Grippe. It seems fatal this winter."

A most unusual endorsement came from Edna Leville of St. Stephen who, from Cottage Craft materials supplied by Nell, made a costume that she entered in the 1923 St. Stephen Winter Carnival. The features of the costume were a dress, tied at the waist, made from two hand woven blankets, fastened at each side with balls of different coloured yarn, each about the size of an egg. Over her shoulders Edna wore a pink blanket, folded from the corners, with more than fifty balls of wool of all colours hanging around the edges. Her face was masked. The banner she made from a yardstick covered with odds and ends of homespun to which she attached a board on which she painted "Char. Co. Cottage Craft." She held the banner high so that all should see it, whether they wanted to or not. Edna won the first prize of $4 for the best original costume, but her real reward, which she repeated several times in a detailed three-page letter, came from winning for Miss Mowat: "I knew I had a good costume, but did not expect to win with so much competition, but for your sake more than my own I am glad that I did.' And to end: 'You are the one to get the credit...For your sake I was glad to win."

No one was more appreciative of Nell's effort to extract art from country living than Stella Jane Smith, an educated and well-read farm wife from Pomeroy Ridge. Born on the Mascarene shore near St. George, Stella had attended the Fredericton Normal School. She took a job teaching school at Pomeroy Ridge and there met and married Charles Smith. Making hooked rugs was her passion. She revelled in the challenge of making them for a wide, sophisticated market and also enjoyed the correspondence between herself and Nell. "Thank you Miss Mowat," she wrote in March 1924, "for writing me such long letters." In response to a request for a rug that Nell hoped to take with her to an exhibition in London, England, Stella wrote: "Tell me when you will want the rug if you go — and if you don't go I shall enjoy doing it for the sake of creating something — I have been helping my girlfriends fill their hope chests this winter. Better political economy to get a young couple married than to cover the world with rugs, but all the time I wish I were doing something I liked instead of making quilts, dresses, etc., which I despise." In another letter, she added, "If you do not take it with you I shall not be offended. It adds a zest to my life that I needed: just to make them and wonder if you will like them, and when I finish one I feel as relieved as if I had had a baby!!! When I am doing one I feel something akin to an artist because *I look just as untidy as Rosa Bonheur's pictures*, to say nothing of the state the house is in. It's lucky I don't have one in the frame all the time." Rosa Bonheur (1822-99) was a French painter of animals and an outspoken feminist who smoked cigarettes and wore trousers.

Nell's homilies about the need to look at nature had found a receptive audience: "Old mother Nature is a changeable jade and trying to catch her colours and not finding them for five minutes the same I discovered why she was given the 'less contrary' sex." Stella was particularly concerned about an authentic blue colouring for the trees. As a farm wife with "seven to be fed and washed and ironed and swept after," she lived vicariously through Nell: "When you go to England, look at the hedge rows and lanes, the ivy and cathedrals for me — Perhaps they are as pretty in my fancies as in reality." With Nell she could also indulge her fancies. In a playful aside, Stella wrote: "Charlotte County is a place down in the far end of New Brunswick where the rocks are so plentifully bestowed by Nature that there is not room for them side by side and they have to be stood on end and where the roads are so crooked that a tall man could not lie down on one and have room to straighten his legs." Her early letters begin formally, "My Dear Miss Mowatt," but later ones she addresses to "My Dear Friend" and signs them "Stella Jane." Late in March 1924, she beseeched Nell to forget business for a while and come and stay: "I've told you before that you should live near me and I should think by now you would realize it. Seriously I wish you would come up by and by when your business slackens...and try and gain some flesh — I think you could stand it. You looked to me as though the pace were killing and I hate to see you look that way. Think it over."

Nell's practice of showing Cottage Craft goods at exhibitions had brought recognition in the world of crafts and this in turn led to reports in national newspapers and magazines. A week or two after the wonderful party in the Foresters Hall in March 1922, *Maclean's*, Canada's national magazine, published a feature article called "Back to the Days of Cottage Craft: The Story of Helen G. Mowat and How She Succeeded in Expanding $10 to $12,000." There is no record of how Gertrude E.S. Pringle first contacted Nell, but she clearly visited St. Andrews, conducted a thorough interview, toured Chestnut Hall and Beech Hill, and perhaps even visited a crafter or two in the county. From her pen we have our first portrait of the adult Nell: "This daughter of loyal descent is of medium height, slight in build, full of energy and vivacity, with very blue eyes set wide apart, piquant, irregular features and a pleasing expression." The story also included photographs of Cottage Craft products, the earliest we have, and descriptions of six different embroidered bags, as well as an embroidered scarf and a hooked rug. The dramatic expansion of her capital, which so impressed Pringle and her editor, was explained this way: "Seven years ago Helen G. Mowat... [was] possessed of the small capital of $10.00...Last year she paid her workers more than $12,000; more than $1,400 was expended on materials, and her total operations were close on $15,000." Nell herself was equally amazed to be dealing in five figures. The entire *Maclean's* article was reprinted in the *St. Croix Courier* on March 23, so all the crafters could share in the glory of being associated with an enterprise that merited national attention, and local people in general be made aware that something truly interesting was happening among them. The world at large had said so, in print.

The regularity and dispatch with which articles such as the *Maclean's* piece were reprinted in the local weekly newspapers suggests that Nell was becoming adept as a publicist. In those days there was a fairly easygoing attitude among editors about the reprinting of brief accounts, and for major or feature articles permission to reprint would be sought, and usually granted, by an informal phone call. If Nell or one of her friends supplied a clipping of the original report to the editor of the *St. Andrews Beacon* or the *St. Croix Courier*, there was a good chance he would use it. This was the beginning of a publicity pattern that went on for some years; it depended, of course, on the ability of Nell and the crafters to do first-class, newsworthy work.

But recognition did not always come in the form of articles in national magazines. Mrs. Harry M. Bell (née Eva Brownrigg) formerly

Performance of the "Spinning Wheel Song." Courtesy of the Charlotte County Archives

of Oak Bay but in 1923 living in Blueslide, Washington, had made embroidered bags for Nell. She wrote to Nell at the end of a tour through several western states:

> Travelling through the states since last August ... I have been in different needle Craft stores, I would say to my husband "that work don't come up to Miss Mowat's," they would sometimes answer are you from the east I would say "yes." They would ask the question "Do you know Miss Mowat" I would answer "Yes." They said I would love to see her needle craft shop it must be lovely, we read about her in 3 different magazines. The "Modern Priscilla," the *Needle Art,* I have forgotten the other book. They sure enjoying reading your work and life. Mr and Mrs Leaster lives near me, and they are going touring on the 10th of May of this year and one place she said she was going was to Miss Mowat's "Cottage Craft Shop" I have told what a beautiful place it was.

National attention would have been a pipe dream at the outset of the business nine years earlier, but when the opportunity arose for exposure overseas, Nell, clearly brimming with confidence, seized it. The occasion was the 1924 British Empire Exhibition at Wembley in London, referred to in the letter by Stella Smith. (Nell had asked her to hook a rug that she might display at the exhibition and for Stella, brought up on English literature, it was a mouth-watering prospect. Stella loved English stories above all others because, as she put it, they were so "finished.") Nell's vehicle for getting space in the Canadian Pavilion was the beleagured G.G. Ommanney, head of the CPR's Department of Colonization and Development who, still occupied with Nell's flax and pottery projects, asked if, in correspondence, she would not refer to all three subjects in the same letter.

Nell's original application for space in the Canadian Pavilion, made at the beginning of February for an international exhibition to be staged in April, not surprisingly, had been turned down. Two weeks after her initial application, she received a telegram from Major Ommanney telling her that not only had space been found in the Canadian Pacific Pavilion, an annex to the main building, but that a reservation for Cottage Craft exhibits had been made on a ship sailing from Saint John on February 29. She would follow on the SS *Minnedosa* sailing from Saint John on April 2. Nell would have to pay her own fare of $130, but the exhibits would travel courtesy of the CPR. Whether she had complained directly to Major Ommanney, or whether a CPR executive had put pressure on the Canadian commission, is not known. The following day Nell replied, informing him that she would be sending a cask of pottery and boxes of woollens weighing in total about 250 pounds. The director of exhibits would receive the Cottage Craft products and they would be installed in the Canadian Pacific Pavilion by, as Major Ommanney phrased it, "our own Mr. Bruce," under Nell's written and sketched instructions. She herself would not arrive until April 12. In her letter, she must have asked if he could also arrange to have her passport renewed. This, too, Major Ommanney did. It was yet another instance, as Mary Gove Carson would have said, of Nell often getting what she wanted.

But she had not finished with Major Ommanney. In a letter, he referred to a farm scene that was not included in Nell's original inventory. The farm scene was an afterthought that she had decided she would take with her when she sailed in early April. It was to be made of wool and combining weaving, hooking, and embroidery, would represent the Charlotte County countryside on a May morning. If it could be arranged, all the Cottage Craft workers would contribute something. At the exhibition a placard above the scene would read: "This model of a New Brunswick farm is made all of wool by the people who live on these farms." To mount the scene, Nell informed him that she would need a vertical panel, three by three feet, resting on a shelf eighteen inches wide, the whole to be enclosed in a showcase. In his reply, Major Ommanney confirmed that Mr. Bruce would arrange for the making of the case and that the obliging CPR would defray the cost. Nell, however, would have to make the scene to the specifications agreed on, as the dimensions of the showcase could not be changed.

At the exhibition Nell attended her stall and elaborated on the farm scene and the other Cottage Craft products to interested passers-by from Britain and the Empire. She was pleased with the British press notice for the Cottage Craft display:

> In a modest case in the corner of the Canadian Pacific
> Pavilion, there is a display of craftwork and pottery
> which is the work of the women of St Andrew's [*sic*],
> New Brunswick. It is one of the most sincere efforts
> in the Exhibition to give the character of an overseas
> corner of the Empire, leaving that character true to its
> natural habitat, and without the influence or condi-
> tions of the old world. They felt that they were a new
> people in a new world, and that they must produce
> pottery and weaving which would express their own
> landscape and the spirit of their own pioneering. Thus
> the women of New Brunswick have created a national
> art for Canada... Their pottery and rugs seem to have

sunshine imprisoned within them, and the personality
of the landscape lives around the jars and on the plates
which these women have sent to show the right hand of
the Empire that the left hand is not idle.

A Canadian visitor to the exhibition, Marguerite L. Hubbell, included a slide of the Cottage Craft exhibit in *Wembley and the British Empire Story*, an illustrated brochure that she sold at her lectures and slide shows when she returned to Canada. She travelled from Newfoundland to the Pacific coast and wrote to Nell from the Palliser Hotel in Calgary, noting that Nell's was the only exhibit of cottage industries in the Canadian section of the exhibition.

At home, Nell also spread the word about Cottage Craft through lectures to the Women's Canadian Clubs. When teaching at the Halifax Ladies College, she had discovered that although she didn't like the classroom, she was very much at ease before adult audiences. Three different Women's Canadian Clubs invited her to address them about her Cottage Craft work in 1922. On April 27 (about one week after the arrival of the Kanes), she spoke at an evening meeting of the club in St. Stephen. Three weeks later, she went to Saint John where, on Loyalist Day, she was very warmly received as the guest speaker at a luncheon meeting of the Women's Canadian Club in the Royal Hotel. From Saint John she went on to Moncton to give a repeat performance at the Women's Canadian Club there. The content of her Canadian Club lectures was always the same: the founding of Cottage Craft, the need for a native Canadian art and, related to this, the importance of place in both life and art. She also exhibited the range of Cottage Craft products: homespun bags, hooked mats, pottery, embroidered landscapes, and carved walking sticks. The Women's Canadian Clubs were a natural outlet for her, and for the clubs, Nell was a tailor-made speaker. The clubs existed to promote Canada's connection to Britain and Nell, of course, was a fervent Loyalist. She spelled out her credo in her 1924 interview with Norman Rankin of the CPR's publicity department: "I am, first, an enthusiastic New Brunswicker; then, a staunch and loyal Canadian, and finally, an

Cottage Craft parade float promoting farm life, circa 1927.
The roof of the house is a Cottage Craft tweed; inside
but not visible in the photograph are ducks.

Courtesy of the Charlotte County Archives

ardent imperialist." In that same interview, she remarked: "I would
not live anywhere else; this is my home; these are my people — the
finest, most honest and kind in the world."

On 4 May 1922, the *St. Croix Courier* gave a full report of the
St. Stephen meeting:

> The Women's Canadian Club held its regular meeting
> in the town council rooms Thursday evening last, the
> president, Mrs. F. V. Sullivan, in the chair. The regular
> business of the month was transacted, after which
> Mrs. Sullivan, in a graceful manner, introduced Miss
> Helen Mowat of St. Andrews, who was the speaker of
> the evening. Miss Mowat gave a very interesting and
> enlightening address on "Cottage Craft work." She
> spoke of how an appreciation of beauty, art, and a real
> art in Canada which was typically Canadian. She spoke
> of how an appreciation of beauty was being awakened
> and developed in the people which would in time make

Canada much richer in art. Her address was not only most enjoyable but it was in spirit both instructive and patriotic.

The Saint John paper, the *Telegraph-Journal*, served up similar fare:

> COTTAGE CRAFTS OF CHARLOTTE COUNTY
> Miss Helen Mowat Addresses [on Loyalist Day, May 18] Women's Canadian Club in St. John and Exhibits Samples of Art.
>
> Miss Mowatt, who was warmly applauded when she rose to speak, said it meant more to her when her own people, the people of New Brunswick, were interested in her work... Now she had what she called a factory of twenty square miles... and more than 100 women working at the handcraft. Her own home was no longer big enough for the headquarters of the industry and she had taken an old house in St. Andrews and made it over to suit her needs. She could no longer keep in touch with the individual workers except through big meetings twice a year. One grand meeting had been held last year when she returned from Toronto and she had been able to tell the workers that real artists in Toronto had come to see their work and been greatly pleased with it.

Cottage Craft may have been Nell's livelihood, but her larger ambition was to support farm and country life and, as with the display in Wembley, to promote the value of both. Her vehicles for promoting rural and farm life locally were the parade and the pageant. Parades were a prominent feature of St. Andrews life and were held whenever there was an anniversary or, in times of war, a victory to celebrate. Cottage Craft would usually enter a float that advertised not only the work of its knitters and weavers but the virtues of farm and country life in general. More ambitious than floats in the town parades, however, were the summer pageants that Nell organized at Beech Hill between 1922 and 1925.

Modelled loosely after English folk dancing festivals, these pageants celebrated country life and communal practices. Cottage Craft itself was perceived as a community of contented crafters, working in, as Nell was fond of saying, a smokeless factory. At the pageants, the rituals of work, such as mowing, haying, and milking, were conducted in concert, while dancing on the stage was line rather than pair, or couple, dancing. Singers also sang in groups, not individually. No one was left out, either at work or play. "This was real dancing," the *St. Croix Courier* reported: "Something of nature had got into it. It made one feel all sophisticated dancing was an abomination." Mr. Surette, a teacher of music and a spectator at one of the pageants, evoked the setting and the serious intent in a letter to his students:

> Overlooking a field near a farmhouse within sight of the sea, we sat ourselves down with two hundred or more people [most from the summer colony] on a bank covered with hay and facing a platform. Around it were animals, a calf, a horse, hens and chickens, and two batches of rabbits. Soon a procession of men and women appeared in the distance singing to the leadership of two men playing violins. All these people were in farming costume, the men wearing overalls and straw hats of the haymaking sort. They ranged themselves on the platform and proceeded to sing and dance for an hour. The songs were all folk songs from the British Islands, and the dances were those of their ancestors which they sing and dance for their own pleasure in the long winter evenings...One of the songs was about their own occupations, and while one group sang the other proceeded to carry on the occupation; one fed the calf, children fed the rabbits, one woman worked

Spinning Wheel Song

When safely the harvest is stored in the barn,
    'Tis then we make ready for spinning the yarn;
When summer is over and winter is near,
    The song of the wheel is the sound that you hear.

Chorus: Oh this is the song that the spinning wheel
        sings;
        You soon will need mufflers and mittens and
        things,
        So draw a long thread with each turn of the
        wheel
        And double and twist it with spindle and reel.

When flowers are faded and swallows are fled.
    And trees on the hillside are yellow and red,
When mornings are frosty and evenings are long,
    'Tis then that we sing you our spinning wheel song.

Soon over the mountain the snow drifts will come
    And settle down deep round the door of our home,
With mufflers and mittens how warm will we feel
    And value the yarn that was spun on the wheel.

Song of the Loom

Fly, fly, my shuttle, fly, the shades of night are creeping,
And with thy gliding, shifting thread
Our hands must weave the children's bread,
So low, so high, while they lie sleeping. Fly, fly, fly!

Sing, sing, my busy loom, there's music in thy humming
The skein is long, the wool is fine,
And time or chance shall not untwine,
So sing, so sing good fortune's coming. Sing, sing, sing!

Turn, little bobbin, turn, the moments fast are flying,
No wandering thought our work shall spoil, .
He knows not rest who knows not toil.
So turn, so turn, our need supplying, turn, turn, turn!

"Spinning Wheel Song" and "Song of the Loom."
Courtesy of the Ross Memorial Museum

Milking and haymaking at a Cottage Craft summer pageant.
Courtesy of the Charlotte County Archives

Irene Castle stepping out at a summer pageant.
Courtesy of the Charlotte County Archives

at a spinning wheel, and another churned, men mowed the hay, pitched it into the wagon and drove off. The dancing was a thing of beauty, quite perfect in rhythmic motion, and completely free from self-consciousness.

One of the most popular choral numbers, written by Nell herself and performed each year, was the "Spinning Wheel Song," which was accompanied by spinners at their wheels and by young girls throwing winding yarn and tossing balls of wool:

When safely the harvest is stored in the barn,
'Tis when we make ready for spinning the yarn;
When summer is over and winter is near,
The song of the wheel is the sound that you hear.
Oh, this is the song that the spinning wheel sings:
You will soon need mufflers and mittens and things,
So draw a long thread with each turn of the wheel
And double and twist it with spindle and reel!

Another popular song was "Land and Sea" in which choruses of boys and girls alternately sang the praises of both. Girls bearing apple blossoms for spring, bright flowers for summer, goldenrod for autumn, and snow-covered spruce boughs for winter represented the four seasons. As a symbol of the sea, boys dragged a fish-laden seine across the stage.

A country pageant staged within sight of Passamaquoddy Bay could hardly have ignored fishing and the sea, but Nell was fundamentally a landswoman. At times she wrote wistfully of the Bay, the tides, and the rocky shores, but the appeal of these seems to have been purely aesthetic. Fishing and the fishing villages do not figure at all in her writings and only very seldom in Cottage Craft motifs. In the "Bay of Fundy," a poem she wrote for children, she seized on her first opportunity to move inland: "And up the inland rivers, that seek the fundy tides / A pleasant land of apple trees and happy homes abides." Her vision of the ideal life and landscape was essentially the eighteenth century Georgian or Arcadian one that the Loyalists had hoped to create in the Maritimes: a land of small farms, a contented populace, and peaceful villages crowned by Anglican church spires. The sea was too unruly and fishing too hazardous and unpredictable.

After the stage performances, girls and boys served tea in the garden, and prizes for dancing were awarded. The 1924 pageant saw Norman Rankin of the CPR publicity department — probably summoned by Nell — on the grounds taking notes for future copy, along with Mr. Alexander of the *Associated Press and News*, who took a film of the dancers. But the most famous celebrity to attend one of Nell's pageants was Irene Castle of dance and fashion fame. In the summer of 1927, accompanied by her small daughter, Barbara, and a pet mongoose, she rented a house, Cory Cottage, near the Algonquin hotel. The mongoose she wore around her neck when shopping on Water Street. She danced at the Algonquin casino and made a cameo guest appearance at the Beech Hill summer pageant that year. Although an exponent of pair dancing, the informality of country dancing appealed to her, as did the casualness of peasant dress. A disciple of Isadora Duncan, she jettisoned corsets in favour of loose fitting clothing in which women were free to dance and also play tennis, golf, and croquet. Farm and country women were relatively unburdened by bourgeois inhibitions and, as if to acknowledge this, Irene Castle had no reservations about appearing on stage at Beech Hill and, to judge from photographs, enjoying the country dances.

The driveway at Beech Hill, as described in one of
Nell's letters to Bliss Carman. Courtesy of Basil Lowery

"Countess of Charlotte"

Comfortably housed in Chestnut Hall, with a reliable staff and well-organized teams of craft workers, Cottage Craft, by the end of the 1920s no longer needed Nell's constant attention. In 1928, she had acquired another invaluable aide: the adventurous and resourceful Frances Wren, daughter of Captain Ranby Wren, a St. Andrews native with a distinguished record in both the merchant marine and the Royal Navy. Under Nell's guidance, Frances tackled all kinds of creative work in drawing, painting, and crafts. She had what one writer described as "a Puckish, elfin talent," partly because she herself was not very tall, but mainly because her drawings often revealed a wry wit. For some years she was the main retail clerk for Cottage Craft during the tourist season, doing art or craft work between customers. She was very appreciative of Nell's teaching and encouragement: "With Miss Mowat around, life was always interesting, no matter what you were doing! She regarded everyone around her as a person — not just an employee. She tried to broaden our interests and help us enjoy life."

The stock market crash in 1929, and the economic depression that followed, left Cottage Craft unscathed. Against all expectations, the depression appears to have strengthened rather than weakened tourism in New Brunswick. The rich and the middle classes continued to travel. Henry Ford's introduction of the Model T, an automobile that anyone with a good salary could afford, allowed middle-class families, who might have balked at rail travel, to travel at will. The provincial government's Bureau of Information and Tourist Travel (established in 1926) reported that motor tourist traffic from the US in 1930 was 44 percent greater than the previous year. Individual expenditures were down slightly, but tourism revenues overall were greater. Travellers from other parts of Canada also poured into New Brunswick, four or five times as many of them in 1930 as in 1927, according to government estimates. The trend persisted. At the end of the 1934 tourist season, hotels, summer resorts, and roadside cabins throughout the province, according to the *St. Croix Courier*, reported that traffic was not only greater in volume than in other seasons but also of much better quality.

As southern New Brunswick's leading resort, St. Andrews attracted much of the increased traffic. In 1934, Harry Wiley, the proprietor of "Wiley's Historic View" log cabins, overlooking Dochet's Island on the St. Croix River a few miles above St. Andrews, reported doing a "rushing business" all summer and that the travellers "seem to have money to spend." In the fall of 1937, the owners of the "Seaside Inn" on Water Street began building a new promenade, bathing huts, and a diving platform. Back-to-back Sun Life Insurance conventions (separated by one day) at the Algonquin in September 1936, each with 400 delegates, required McQuoid's taxi service on Water Street to keep forty cars on call day and night. Many of these cars were privately owned and had been hired for the occasion, along with their drivers. Ancillary businesses also benefited. In 1932, R.J. Conley, the owner of a lobster factory on Market Square (which would become the postwar home of Cottage Craft) began building a pound for 600,000 lobsters on Deer Island to supplement an existing pound one third that size. The lobsters were trucked to cities and resorts on the eastern seaboard.

As well as encouraging Frances Wren to broaden her interests, Nell, at this time, attended to her own. Interests that the demands of business had kept her from pursuing as much as she would had have liked, she could now cultivate. As a young woman, painting and drawing, on which as a teacher her livelihood had depended, may have had first claim on her attention, but as she aged, they were rivalled by writing as a craft. In February 1914, when Cottage Craft was in its infancy, she wrote what, in effect, was a fan letter to Fredericton-born Bliss Carman, who was then living in New Canaan, Connecticut. Bliss Carman, at fifty-three, was eastern Canada's most celebrated poet and until his retreat to Connecticut, he had worked in New York as a syndicated news-

Bliss Carman
Archives & Special Collections, Harriet Irving Library, University of New Brunswick (Rufus Hathaway Photograph Collection, Bliss Carman, no. 3)

paper columnist and as a writer and editor for a number of magazines, among them *Atlantic Monthly* and *Cosmopolitan*. In his reply to Nell, then thirty-nine, he confessed that he had never been to St. Andrews but that his sister was a fairly frequent visitor and had spoken to him of its attractiveness. (Jean Murray Carman was married to W.F. Ganong, the St. Stephen-born naturalist, historian, and chair of botany at Smith College in Northampton, Massachusetts.)

The content of Nell's letter can only be inferred from his reply. He refers to a walk on snowshoes — to a crossroads mailbox — that had been Nell's platform for a paean of praise to the winter landscape. In Carman, she would find an appreciative reader. He, too, was fond of winter's stillness and the pared-down quality that exposed each branch and twig. The summer landscape, by contrast, was overdressed and shapeless. He asked Nell if she had read Emerson's "Snowstorm" and he praised the independence of her mind: "I never knew anyone else who dared to call summer monotonous. But it is. People are betrayed by the appeal to the luxurious senses in June. Winter's rare

heroism of spirit escapes them." He also chided Nell good-naturedly
for her shyness about writing to authors: "Don't you ever be undecid-
ed about writing to authors! Do it! And tell them you have enjoyed
their writings. They like it. It helps them. It makes them feel they are
not wholly useless in the world. The really big ones are inundated
with letters, I suppose. But the smaller men and 'minor' poets very
seldom receive letters from strangers. At least that is my experience.
One lone reader is like a spring in the desert."

His second letter, written in December 1914 in response to a
poem sent by Nell, he addressed to "My Dear Lady Beech Hill."
The poem, he thought, "isn't bad;" it had atmosphere and the virtue
of simplicity. He did, however, think that, from a mistaken sense of
economy, she might have run two poems into one. He suggested that
she divide the subjects and write two separate poems: one about a
portrait and the other about memories of a garden that the portrait
had triggered. Carman found Nell's treatment of the garden too long
and too distracting. "You show me a portrait, and before I have time
to really see it, you place over it a painting of an old garden, and hide
the portrait entirely. You say I can see a garden in a dream confined?
Then you go into a trance and describe it, and leave me standing with
the first two stanzas awaiting completion. You see I know all about it,
for my own early poems are full of just such confusion of visions." He
then indulged in a vision of his own, imagining Nell writing at a desk
before an open fireplace with brass-handled fire tools and beside it a
window looking down a slope.

In his third letter, written on April 15, 1915, Bliss Carman
addressed Nell as "My Dear Friend." His mood had been darkened
by the war in Europe, a "heinous tragedy," and he regarded his letter to Nell as a "happy task to lighten the suspense of these dark
days of the world." The poem that Nell had sent him, "The Sand
Reef Light," he found "truly capital. It is really masterly in its quiet
and simple faithfulness, and its sweetness of spirit — all as true as
Kipling's 'Sussex,' one of my favourites of his poems." High praise
for a fledgling poet! In particular, he admired Nell's reliance on direct
observation, a principle that Nell would shortly lay down for her

crafters. For their subjects they were to look to their own woods, farms, and fields, not pattern books and magazines. So with her own poems. He liked the fact that "Sand Reef Light" was not "inspired from books at second hand." The ostensible evidence of this was Nell's use of words and phrases peculiar to her locality — "sentinel," "herring weir," "creeper boughs" — that were not common in literature. But no sensitive reader, he added, would need this endorsement of the poem's originality and of the poet's attachment to her place. He drew attention to particular words and phrases that Nell might amend but overall he considered the poem to be authentic and charming, and quite "magazine-able," even if it was a little too long. He ended the letter with a reference to a romance or story that Nell had proposed writing from some historical material she had unearthed. He thought she might do something admirable with it if she could piece it out and write it as simply as she wrote to him — with as evident sincerity and lack of effort. The romance, Carman surmised, was a life story, perhaps a tragic one, covering a long term of years. He encouraged her to treat it at length, "not a short story, as short stories are always in a hurry and the flavour of old times is always lost in a hurry. Let it be as long as it needs to be."

This same advice about writing without contrivance had been delivered indirectly by Nell's cousin Owen Campbell more than twenty years earlier. Owen always enjoyed Nell's letters: "you have more talent for writing naturally than most people. That is to say you are able to write a good deal as you talk." Owen's opinion was endorsed by his fiancée, Sylla, to whom Owen read aloud at least one of Nell's letters. Playfully, Owen also noted that if Nell's talent for flirting was at all commensurate with her talent for letter writing St. Andrews would not afford the seventeen-year-old Nell her proper scope.

Nell's association with Bliss Carman continued until his death in 1929. He wrote to her on the death of her mother and after the death of his own sister in 1920. Nell confided to him the nervous collapse that, in that same year, prompted her visit to England at the height of the tourist season. He expressed interest in the work of Nell's crafters and asked if she knew of Helen Albee's rug weaving cooperative in New Hampshire, which he thought must be a sister enterprise. He had read, and liked, Albee's book *The Gleam*, a history of her personal and spiritual development. However taxing the demands of Cottage Craft, he urged Nell not to abandon her Muse: "Hold on to poetry with one hand, while you needle-work with the other."

Her request, in 1923, that he read selections of his prose and verse to the Women's Canadian Club at St. Andrews initiated another lively exchange of letters, and one of increased warmth. In March 1923, after she wrote to ask if covering his expenses would be sufficient, she was "Dear Miss Mowat," but after his visit in June, she was "My dear Countess of Charlotte," even though Nell had talked him out of his usual fee and subjected him to her driving. The prospect of travelling by car in Charlotte County had filled Bliss with apprehension: "Motor cars in N.B. are quite outside my imagining. I could as easily fancy visiting King Arthur's court in an auto, or the Vale of Tempe. However — it is never too late to be jolted out of one's youthful prejudices. So — I...lay my life in your hands — only *not* over twenty miles an hour." Although he objected to the "roadmasters" who covered the red roads with grey, St. Andrews and Charlotte County did not disappoint: "You were quite right about Charlotte County. It certainly has a strength and loveliness and charm all its own, which do not let the traveller forget them." Of St. Andrews, whose coastal setting and white-painted buildings climbing the slope behind, reminded him of a Greek colonial city, he wrote: "My first glimpse of St. Andrews from the American side was never to be forgotten. It was like a scene from the ancient world of Hellas as I have imagined it." A recent batch of Nell's poetry, too, came in for high praise: "The verses in themselves are excellent, very felicitous and not strained, and as always with your things full of the breath of our country. No alien could have written 'Clear as the voice of melting snow.'"

Bliss Carman's visit clearly had been a triumph and Nell would have been able to reassure her friend Kim Osburn, who, while acknowledging the writer's acceptance of Nell's invitation to speak in St. Andrews as another instance of Nell's proverbial good luck, was apprehensive about the meeting. Kim had written: "I hope Bliss Carman was a great success, things come your way almost uncannily, but I wonder if he came up to expectations, authors so seldom do."

Kate Reed, the chief decorator of all CPR hotels and passenger ships, confirmed Bliss's affection for Nell in a letter written from Winnipeg in January 1927. Kate and Hayter Reed owned a house in St. Andrews immediately below the Algonquin and had used their influence to help Nell raise capital for her pottery venture. She met Bliss Carman in her favourite book shop in Winnipeg and, as she wrote Nell, once a St. Andrews connection had been made, "[I] wasn't long in telling him that you and I were friends. You should have seen his dear face light up, and the flood gates were opened…Then when we were parting I said 'I hope you will come to us the next time you come to St. Andrews' and he said 'Oh, no! I must go to my old friend Nellie.' You can," she concluded warmly, "get into the eternities instantly with him."

Nell, of course, felt equally fond of Bliss Carman and she conveyed her regard for him, and the debt she owed to his poetry, in a verse of her own that she sent to him in 1923. For Nell, who had known only English poets, Bliss's was a familiar and reassuring northern voice:

TO BLISS CARMAN
But one with a voice more kindly gracious
Sang me songs that I seemed to know
Sang of my familiar places
With the wild clear voice of the melting snow

Sang me songs of the April showers,
Sang me songs of the Fundy tides,
Songs of the wild geese and wayside flowers
And scarlet maples on mountain sides

. . . .

When had he known our Northern gladness?

Whence had he wandered so far away?
Would in his heart no touch of sadness
Bid him turn and come back some day?
....
Then it was that my heart's desire
Came like a dream from the faded past
One day I found by my own hearth fire
That truant poet come home at last.

In 1928, Ru-Mi-Lou Books of Ottawa published *Funny Fables of Fundy*, a collection of illustrated rhymes and verses, chiefly for children. It was Nell's first published book. Nell was very fond of children, Mady Holmes (the daughter of Boyd Merrill) recalling that when she was young Nell read to her every night, sitting around the register in the hall. Nell loved A.A. Milne, and so did Mady. Mady also posed for some of the drawings in *Funny Fables* and acquired from Nell the habit of sitting with one leg tucked under her. The other children would say to Mady, "Come on, get up Nellie." *Funny Fables*, which Nell dedicated to William Brodie, "my old schoolmaster," brought her a great deal of recognition. The poet Sir Charles G.D. Roberts wrote to tell her that he was "delighted" with the fables: "such delightfully quaint, unexpected turns of mood and phrase, — such delicious humour never over-strained or self-conscious, — and every here and there such flashes of essential poetry. The book is unique and I expect it to *live*, with the immortal *Alice* and with *A Child's Garden of Verses*, but utterly unlike to either." Bliss Carman was equally enthusiastic: "It wins the highest praise everywhere, and fills everyone who reads it with delight... It is a masterpiece in every way. Has ease and felicity, fine humor, and a very sound content good for grownups as well as children." He thought that Nell's book would do well in the US and offered to recommend it to his publishers, Dodd, Mead & Co, in "the strongest terms."

Although the poems were written ostensibly for children, Nell, who was fiercely protective of her person and her place, had no scruples about using some of them as platforms from which to attack people who she felt had wronged her, or projects of which she disapproved. Two of the poems fall into Mary Gove Carson's category of Nell's "little sermons."

Book cover for *Funny Fables of Fundy*.
Blue Heron Printing, 1990

The most unsparing of these, "Bird Law," refers to a lawsuit against Minnie Denley who had worked as a housekeeper at Beech Hill. In June 1924, after her return from another visit to England, Nell found several articles missing from the house. Suspecting Minnie Denley, and armed with a warrant, she searched the apartment of the Denleys who were now living with their new employers, Mr. and Mrs. Dalgleish. On finding a number of items that she claimed were her own, Nell appealed to the Grand Jury, which found a true bill, and subjected Minnie Denley to a three-day trial in September 1925. Nell may have championed the farm folk of Charlotte County, but she looked down on the Denleys, describing Minnie, who had worked for her for five years, as "always troublesome, jealous and discontented and a low grade of mentality."

She had some difficulty in persuading the police to prosecute and in finding a solicitor who would take the case. A request to John Power of the Saint John police department that he recommend a detective who — at her expense — would handle the case for her was gently rebuffed on grounds that the police department did not undertake private commissions. Nor, partly on the grounds of expense, could he recommend a detective from outside the department who might act for her. He suggested instead that she apply to the local magistrate for a search warrant. Lawyers, too, were no less reluctant to take the case. Three, P.E. McLaughlin, R.B. Harmon, and H.M. Groom, either declined or were so dilatory that Nell, boiling with impatience, looked elsewhere. Harry Groom asked, first, if she had witnesses who could identify the allegedly stolen items or who could testify that they had seen the items in the presence of Mrs. Denley, and, second and most pointedly, "will these people come willingly and give evidence?" Harry Groom, from St. Stephen, understood the dynamics of small communities.

Why Nell pressed charges, in the absence of any damning or compelling evidence, is puzzling. There is a clue in a letter from her friend Kim Osburn Wait (now married to Dick Wait) in Somerville, Massachusetts. Nell, she noted, liked drama: "We're bursting to know how the trial came out. I do wish I could have been there — I know it must have been better than any play. I hope it's ended now one way or another. It has kept you stirred up so long. However I know you thrive on a little excitement. I always wonder what new and original project you'll be absorbed in when I next see you — one year its founding an industry — then vamping the parson — then reforming the legal system...and oh, I forgot your little contretemps with the customs."

Mr. and Mrs. Dalgleish, whose support Nell characterized as "a mistaken zeal for protecting the deserving poor," postponed a journey to England in order to testify on behalf of Mrs Denley. (When asked how long she had known Miss Mowat, Mrs. Dalgleish replied, "Far too long.") The defence argued that some of the articles in question had been brought from Montreal by Mrs. Denley and that others had been taken by mistake in moving. These items the Denleys offered to return to Miss Mowat. Unconvinced by the prosecution's case, the jury, despite having been vetted by Nell, returned a verdict of not guilty and the judge ordered her to return to the Denleys certain articles, which Nell, claiming that they were hers, had repossessed.

It was a humiliating defeat and one she never forgot. When, a few years later, Earle B. Smith, who had represented Minnie Denley in court, wrote asking for her support in an approaching federal election, Nell replied that if he worked hard and behaved honourably "people will learn to have faith in you and forget that in the days of your youth you supported crime in the county of Charlotte."

In the poem "Bird Law," an undisguised allegory, Nell cast herself as the swallow who has left her nest and Minnie Denley as the allegedly thieving jay. Mrs. Dalgleish became a rich loon who lived in a large nest by the sea and her husband, who managed Sir William Van Horne's model farm at his summer estate, a small English sparrow living in the nest on sufferance. The judge was an impressionable owl, prevailed upon to direct an equally impressionable jury to favour the jay. The principals, of course, were not named but the entire town knew who the birds represented. Writing from Yale, Maurice Davie, a friend and a professor of economics, asked if she wasn't afraid that "everybody will get the point too pointedly...It's quite a slam on the whole gang, even the learned owly judge." The moral of the three-day trial was conveyed in the final stanza:

> Now, children be warned by this tale, which is true,
> The swallow told me and I tell it to you.
> ....
> You cannot have safety and justice and peace,
> With an owl for a judge and a jury of geese.
> And if you want help when enforcing the law,
> Beware of a loon that's protecting the poor!

In "Fundy Tides," Nell's victim was an engineer, Dexter P. Cooper, who dreamed of harnessing the power in Passamaquoddy's huge tidal flows by building dams between the islands at the mouth of the bay. Cooper, who was a friend of Frederick Delano Roosevelt, is said to have conceived of the project while honeymooning on Campobello, but in reality the conception owed much to his collaborator Wallace Rupert Turnbull, the Saint John inventor of the variable pitch propeller.

The loon told the owl, as she drew him aside,
That she knew for a fact that the swallow had lied.

Illustration for the poem "Bird Law."
From *Funny Fables of Fundy*, Blue Heron Printing, 1990

The Cooper-Turnbull plan was to dam the mouths of both the Passamaquoddy and Cobscook bays. Water would be allowed to escape from Passamaquoddy into Cobscook Bay through turbine generators located at Moose Island. In Cobscook Bay, the water would be held until low tide and then released into the Bay of Fundy through a set of gates. During the first Roosevelt administration, dykes were built between Treat Island (Eastport) and Dudley Island (Lubec) and from Pleasant Point Passamaquoddy Reservation out to Carlow Island, Eastport, and then to Moose Island. Congress, however, on grounds of costs and potential environmental damage, refused additional funds and work stopped. To Nell, the prospect of industrial development in Passamaquoddy was anathema. Cities might provide the goods and services without which no small town could survive and, in the case of St. Andrews, the tourists which had been its salvation, but they could get their power elsewhere. In Nell's poem, the tides, angered by the building of the dykes, smash them during an equinoctial gale and sweep the chief protagonist, Dexter P. Cooper, out to sea:

Down, down went the dam and the sea-wall besides,
And the engineer fell with the wreck in the tides.
And the waves washed his pockets as clean as could be
And carried his plans and his gold out to sea

He may have survived, for I know he could swim,
But the tides nevermore have been bothered with him.

In 1932, she followed *Funny Fables* with *The Diverting History of a Loyalist Town*, a romanticized history of St. Andrews based largely on hearsay evidence and documents preserved in her own family. The Loyalists are exalted. George III was a benevolent, misunderstood patriarch and the American rebels, villains. The arrival of the Loyalists — the men in plum-coloured frock coats, wigs, and three corner hats, and the women in quilted petticoats and long, short-waisted dresses — was a "kind of vast picnic."

Painting by Nell for the cover for *The Diverting History of a Loyalist Town.*

Courtesy of Anthony E. Hilditch

It was a scene, she continues, that might have tempted a Watteau or Fortuney. Once landed there was no unseemly competition for appointments and official favours that the Loyalists in general craved, and no haggling and jockeying for the choice commercial lots. Remittance men from England, who came in numbers to Charlotte County, far from being black sheep, were "thoroughbreds," whose gentle manners and soft voices left their mark in remote parts of the county. Most egregious of all in a history that brings us to the end of the nineteenth century is the absence of anything but a fleeting reference to the Irish. By 1871, more than half the town's population was of Irish descent. Nell refers at some length to the St. Andrews-Quebec Railway and expands on the Englishmen who were brought over to manage it, but the builders, the men and boys who levelled the track bed and laid the ties and the rails — undernourished and diseased post-famine Irish emigrants — warrant only a sentence: "We find Squire Wilson sailing over to Ireland and...[returning] home with a load of Irish navvies to work on the railroad." Not a group or a company or even a gang, but a load. There is no mention of the quarantine station on miniscule, treeless Hospital Island, a few miles offshore, nor to groups of ragged, hungry emigrants begging on the streets. According to Nell, St. Andrews was a "very gay and busy place in the early days of the railroad." The book, in short, was less a history than an invention, an exercise — in its treatment of the Loyalists — in hagiography that strengthened and perpetuated a cherished myth.

But as well as exalting the Loyalists, *Diverting History* gave the town the Loyalist label that, when it could no longer market itself as an Elysium of health, enabled it to call upon a distinctive and, if Nell was to be believed, distinguished history. What had been a well preserved old town became, in the importance placed on history or heritage as a tourist attraction after World War II, treasured space. History as well as art, the province and the town realized, could be a cash crop. St. Andrews had no sand beaches and, with the exception of an enclosed lagoon, no warm salt water. It could still offer cool, refreshing air and a virtually mosquito-free environment, but hay fever sufferers and neurasthenics could now get relief from drugs at home. So, to maintain the flow of visitors, Loyalist-built public buildings were restored, old houses were refurbished and equipped with historic plaques, and visitors furnished with maps, pamphlets, and guides of the original town plat, or plan, laid out by British military surveyors in 1783. All of this took decades to achieve but the potential transforming power of *Diverting History* was sensed at once by Thomas H. Marshall, a lawyer from Pittsburgh and a regular visitor to St. Andrews. He ended an emotional letter to Nell with the following tribute: "You have done a great thing for St. Andrews in writing this book and have done so much for the people of the town

A MAD Society painting group, with Nell (wearing hat) seated on the far right. Courtesy of the Charlotte County Archives

in so many ways, that long years after you are dead and gone I shall take great pleasure in suggesting to summer residents that they read your book and thus develop a love for St. Andrews, I shall tell them how 'Nellie Mowat' was known by every person in the town, invited to everything, admired by all who knew her and beloved by all her friends."

Maurice Davie of Yale also recognized Nell's growing celebrity. After reading, and liking, *Funny Fables,* he advised that she cash in on her appeal to readers, if not yet to visitors, by suggesting to her publishers that they "play up *Nellie Mowat* — who she is, what she does, the life she leads, etc. — and that will get people started on buying the book." More than thirty years later, Will R. Bird, in his 1969 book *These are the Maritimes,* returned to these same themes, the beguiling power of Nell's writings on St. Andrews and Nell herself as a tourist attraction: "You buy...Miss Mowat's story of St. Andrews,

Returning from a MAD Society rehearsal.
Courtesy of the Charlotte County Archives

and you'll find we've been giving you the truth. She's the smartest woman in seven counties and you ought to meet her. Maybe you will — head on. If you see a car coming in the middle of the road, pull for the ditch. She's reckless." In 1995, Andrew Sackett, in an illuminating MA thesis, dubbed Nell the architect of modern St. Andrews tourism. Her reconstitution of St. Andrews, he argues, "has become an official orthodoxy which no citizen of, or visitor to, St. Andrews can ignore." *Diverting History* remained in publication until the 1980s and may even, it is rumoured, be published again.

As the Loyalist myth filled more and more of Nell's persona, she became commensurately more anti-American. Despite rewarding years spent in New York and New England, and the kindness of American friends and acquaintances living and summering in St. Andrews, by middle age she could be rudely dismissive of Americans who did not sympathise with the Loyalist cause. While pouring tea at a wedding reception, she is reported to have remarked without a hint of irony, in response to an observation made by the bride's American uncle, that "the only decent tea they ever had over there they dumped in Boston

Harbour." She was, noted Harry Mallory, who overheard the remark about tea dumping, "a great Britisher." On another occasion, she is said to have stepped on an American flag and removed and destroyed all the American magazines from the town library — this while living in a house whose American owners had granted her and her father life tenancy without rent.

Nell's final contribution to the arts in the years before World War II was the creation of a society that would allow people, the young in particular, to exercise their talents in music, art, and drama; in short, a MAD Society. Founded in the fall of 1934, the group put on its first show in March 1935, including two short plays by Nell, *The Perfect Actor* and *Past and Present*. MAD was conceived as a society for women but men could participate in plays that had male characters and they were invited to attend art exhibits, plays, and concerts. At the time of Nell's death, MAD could boast nearly 100 members, and the society would remain active until the 1980s.

Nell standing outside the Hole in the Wall,
Cottage Craft's wartime quarters.

Passing the Torch

Nell's stewardship of Cottage Craft effectively ended with the coming of World War II, and particularly with American involvement after 1941. Gas was rationed, the Algonquin hotel closed, and people everywhere were apprehensive. Few were travelling and few buying. Nell, too, was aging: she was sixty-four at the beginning of the war and seventy at its end. To adjust to a shrinking market, she sold Chestnut Hall to Henry and Sarah Phipps Ross, who later bequeathed the house to the town on condition that it serve as a museum for their collection of furniture and decorative art. The Rosses, who lived at Rossmount, an estate at the foot of Chamcook Mountain, were world travellers and collectors. No longer a mecca for summer tourists, Cottage Craft moved into a tiny shop, the Hole in the Wall, on Water Street, not far from its junction with King, and there it sat out the war. With the defeat of Germany and then Japan, Nell had to consider her own future and the future of the business. It was time to sell. And as fate would have it, and without advertising, along came ideal buyers. Her proverbial luck had not deserted her.

Kent and Evan Burrill (Bill) Ross [no relation to Henry and Sarah Phipps Ross] were recently demobbed servicemen; Kent had been a lieutenant in the navy and Bill a captain in the army. Both had been born in Nova Scotia, Bill in Amherst and Kent, the younger of the two, in Pictou. Before the war both brothers had worked for the Royal Bank of Canada in a number of Maritime towns. Their father, the Reverend William Ross, was a Presbyterian minister and teacher who, after the union of the Presbyterian and Methodist Churches, was appointed principal of Mount Allison Ladies College in Sackville, New Brunswick, a United Church foundation affiliated with the degree-granting Mount Allison College. The Rosses lived there from 1926 to1935, in a spacious apartment on campus, before eventually moving to Halifax. Their mother, Victoria Burrill Ross, had been a pupil of Nell's at the Halifax Ladies College and over the years the two women had become friends. In Victoria Ross's published diary of the Mount Allison years, there is an illuminating exchange with Kent, who had asked why she went to such lengths to reassure the "rookies," the new arrivals. She replied: "One can only judge from one's own experience and that is how it was with me when, at the age of 14, I was put in a boarding school. It was a week before my roommate showed up and I cried myself to sleep every night. The art-teacher Miss Helen Mowat heard me one night and came to comfort me — I've loved her ever since."

Liberated by the war, Bill and Kent had no desire to return to banking and, possibly influenced by their mother's interest in weaving and the arts, their thoughts turned to handcrafts. At Sackville, and later in Halifax, and in their parents' summer place at Pictou, they had grown up with music, books, and paintings. At Mount Allison, there were also regular concerts and art exhibitions. As all parents know, nurture does not always work but in the case of the young Rosses, even though they opted initially for careers in finance, it is reasonable to suppose that their sensibilities were affected by the tastes of cultivated and civilized parents. Bill had also worked for several summers in his uncle's textile factory at Yarmouth, Nova Scotia. Walter Burrill made "duck" fabric used as a liner (of rubber boots, for example) and the experience might have given Bill some feel for the flow of raw materials that goes into the production of a fabric.

On wartime leaves in Nova Scotia, and when driving after the war, they had taken note of roadside signs for handcraft shops and wondered if this offered a possible livelihood. They had never visited St. Andrews, although Bill had seen the enticing view of it across the estuary of the St. Croix when driving on Route 1 from Boston to Halifax. And while they knew of Miss Mowat, they had never met her. In a Christmas letter to Victoria Ross, in 1945, Nell mentioned that she was now seventy and that she was thinking of selling Cottage Craft. After listening to her sons' musings, Victoria wrote to Nell and suggested that she visit her in St. Andrews. Nell

Frances Wren standing outside the Hole in the Wall. Courtesy of the Charlotte County Archives

encouraged her to come, and Mrs. Ross and Kent — who had just been discharged from the navy — drove to St. Andrews to spend a few days with her. Nell must have liked Kent, who was a capable and attractive young man, and Kent must have seen the possibilities in a now near-dormant Cottage Craft. After some negotiation, he and Bill made an offer and during the winter of 1946 they became Cottage Craft's new owners.

Nell had created a profitable business with an international reputation, but she had little in the way of material goods to sell. She had already sold Chestnut Hall, her retail outlet, and the Hole in the Wall was just that, a rented cave with a front window. She would have had some inventory but throughout the war stocks were low. Her real capital was the loyalty and goodwill of the sixty or seventy handcraft workers scattered throughout Charlotte County that she could call upon. It was difficult to put a price on these since her handworkers were not under contract and their looms and other equipment were their own. Bill and Kent Ross's only capital, on the other hand, was a "quite decent" discharge pay, but it could hardly have been munificent. The solution to the conundrum of buyers with little to offer and a vendor with only an organization and a name to sell was the promise of a lifetime pension for Nell. In exchange for Cottage Craft, Bill and Kent handed over whatever capital they could spare ("you'd be surprised how little it was," Bill confided) with the proviso that they would pay Nell a monthly sum for the rest of her life. The debt would die with her. The monthly payments were Nell's pension and they were also, of course, her assurance of a continuing link with Cottage Craft. Bill and Kent were to some degree her guardians and she, albeit at arms length, their mentor. Several times a week, Nell dropped down to the shop to check the work of the outworkers and to offer advice on new patterns and designs. For the Ross brothers, she was "the Boss" for as long as she lived.

For the first year or so under the new regime, Beech Hill was still the production centre for the business and a temporary home for the Rosses. Bill and Kent used the ell at the farm for washing the raw wool and pressing the woven fabric, and for the first winter, Kent and his wife Liz (Mallory) lived in the house. Kent taught himself to weave on a loom in the attic. In February 1947, Bill and Elizabeth also stayed at Beech Hill until they found a house in town. Two features of life at Beech Hill remained in Elizabeth Ross's memory: a driveway that "seemed to go on for miles," and delicious soups that Miss Mowat kept adding to as they were eaten. From Nell, Kent and Bill received instruction in dyeing and in the art of blending coloured yarns. Nell made up her dyes in a copper pot on the wood stove and then experimented with blending different colours of yarn on small hand cards. The cards were her palette and, as Bill Ross remarked, she could do with coloured yarn what painters did with paints. Nell, of course, could also paint.

Living at Beech Hill was a convenient arrangement for the novices, but to support two families they calculated that they would have to do three times as much business as formerly, and this meant year-round facilities for washing the wool and drying the woven yard goods. At Beech Hill, there was not enough water for washing the wool in winter. On the subject of expanding the business, Nell's advice was characteristically forthright: "The only way for you boys to succeed is to add a new line such as clothing."

To get materials for a new washing and drying shed, to be built on a piece of land close to Beech Hill and the town's water line, the Rosses bid successfully on a government building — a former residence for about sixty young women — at the Pennfield RCAF base. The building, which they tore down, had a sound hardwood floor and, as Bill remarked, "the best shingles you could find." There were also hot water radiators, showers, and plumbing and heating equipment that they were able to sell to people in and around town. The sale of these items more than covered the cost of the building and precluded building anew by allowing them to buy a recently vacated lobster plant, which had been a notorious speakeasy in a previous incarnation, on the waterfront at Market Square. With two hired carpenters and two employees, Earle ("Acker") McNab and fourteen-year-old Ellis McLaughlin, they set about converting the former Conley lobster plant into a workshop and retail store. Bill, Kent, and their two helpers did the rough carpentry and the hired carpenters the finishing work. The carpenters built a shop front on the side facing Market Square, using windows from the Pennfield building, while the labourers and rough carpenters brought the washing machine down from Beech Hill and set it up at the back of the building. The upstairs rooms they used for storing yarn. After about a year, they closed the Hole in the Wall and transferred retailing to the Connolly building. Both Bill and Kent loved softwood so they finished the interior of the retail section with pine chiefly and with whatever other attractive material they could find.

Bigger sales meant new markets, as well as new lines, and the Rosses went after these aggressively. At the time of the takeover there was no wholesale trade; within two years, they had persuaded forty gift shops in Canada, the US, and West Indies to carry Cottage Craft

Conley's lobster plant, the postwar home of Cottage Craft.
Courtesy of the Charlotte County Archives

products. There was also the mail order business, as well as the summer retail trade. The Algonquin, which had been closed for five years, reopened, and summer families returned to their boarded-up houses. Train services to St. Andrews, which had also been suspended, were resumed and continued until 1960 when they succumbed to near-universal car ownership.

In the 1950s summer retailing included rented shop space at Fundy National Park where Dr. Ivan Crowell, director of the handicrafts division of the province's Department of Industry and Reconstruction, organized a two-month handcrafts summer school. Individuals and families could attend the school for days or even weeks at a time. A shop in a park that actively promoted handcrafts seemed a potential money-maker, so the Rosses applied to the government for retail space in one of the cabin colonies. The government obliged with space for a shop in an administration building and a bunkhouse for staff.

The Rosses stocked the shop with yarn, embroidered handbags, and boxed tweed sets of yarn and fabric to be made up, judging that families in rented cottages and campers would not want tailored wool garments. Young Bill Ross, Bill and Elizabeth's son, worked at Fundy Park for several summers while he was a student and he slept in the attic of the building where room had been allocated for the shop. He hung his clothes from the rafters. Access to the attic was by a ladder on a pulley that proved challenging even to a young, fit man after an evening at the pub.

To keep up with the continent-wide demand, Bill and Kent had up to seventy-five women outworkers as well as a permanent staff of five in St. Andrews. The brothers divided the work of management according to their talents; Bill looked after the financial side of the business and Kent, broadly speaking, the design and production, but neither function was exclusive and both men liked working out front with the customers. Their different talents were apparent quite early in their lives. After their first day of drawing lessons at the art school in Sackville, Victoria Ross was convinced that neither Bill, then eight, nor his sister Audrey "would ever register in the field of art." Bill's drawings lacked perspective and had "a rakish mobile air" about them. Kent's drawings and sketches, on the other hand, drew accolades. Emily Warren, a visiting associate of the Royal Academy in 1930, when Kent was nine, said of his drawings: "These show real artistic ability — he has a sense of colour and of perspective — his drawing is good." As an adult, Kent had a reputation for being "very artistic" and at Cottage Craft, he was able to apply his feel for colour and design to patterns and colour combinations for tweeds. Victoria Ross also recognized that Kent had "driving-power."

To help with the work of designing, in-house production, and the general running of the store, they hired a young Englishman, Derrick ("Bon") Harriot, who had been introduced to them by Dr. Crowell. Bon came to Rothesay in New Brunswick as a child evacuee from London. He returned to London after the war but came back to Canada to study weaving and design at the provincial government's handicrafts centre in Fredericton. For some months, he also lived at Beech Hill. The local youth, Ellis McLaughlin, also learned to work the blanket loom.

The heavier manual work was the domain of Acker McNab. His main job was to wash, spin dry, and steam press the homespun webs of fabric when they came in from the weavers. He squeezed out the water in a big wringer and pressed the fabric while it was still damp. Washing pre-shrinks and softens the fabric, while pressing it at the correct temperature maintains its integrity. He also put together batches of yarn for the weavers and at times when there were attractive women in the shop he would pretend to be "management," appearing with a pencil and notebook to inspect the stock. Acker also liked his beer and was a very early exponent of the "happy hour." On Friday afternoons anyone boating close to the shore on the east side of the wharf at Market Square might have seen a bag suspended by a rope just at or below the water line. Every Friday morning Acker hung six beers in a burlap bag below his workshop so that by 4:30 pm they would be nicely chilled by the tide. There was a trap door beside the washing machine.

In the shop itself, Bill and Kent assembled, as Bill's wife, Elizabeth, described them, "a wonderful staff." Among the early recruits was Ida Kline, who "was so good with the customers and the craft workers." Shipping was handled by Rita Greenlaw, who was also responsible for keeping track of the dye lot of yarn sent to each weaver so that fabric and yarn could be matched for skirt and sweater combinations. The sweater would be knitted and the skirt made up by, or for, the purchaser. Later, in the 1960s, the Rosses hired the irrepressible and irreverent Mary Janet Clift. One day Mary Janet happened to remark to a friend, "Wouldn't Bill and Kent Ross be the greatest guys to work for!" The friend must have relayed the comment to Kent who rang Mary Janet and asked if she would like to work part-time for Cottage Craft. Mary Janet hesitated on the grounds that she had no experience, whereupon Kent retorted "You can count, can't you!" When on a slack day in winter she confessed that she wasn't earning her keep, Kent asked her to pick the chaff, darker spots, which showed in the live lobster tweed but not in other colours. He took down a bolt, laid out several yards on a counter, and bending over the material with a needle, demonstrated how to flick out the seeds and the bits of grass. When asked, after he had straightened his back, if she could manage this Mary Janet replied, "I'd rather pick the fly shit out of pepper." Kent doubled up again — but this time in mirth. Mary Janet, in her own words, "could sell fridges to Eskimos," but Cottage Craft products were not a hard sell. Her mantra to parting customers was "see you in ten or twenty years. Quality lasts." Mary Janet also won the annual "Foot in Mouth Award" (a display foot with a broken toe) asking one customer who was buying yarn if she was a "knight titter." She worked for Cottage Craft for twenty years. Ida Kline worked for twenty-two years; Rita Greenlaw, twenty-one; and Earle McNab, twenty-five. The Rosses, Rita Greenlaw remarked, "were the most kind people; it was just like family."

To organize the outworkers, Kent and Bill had one forewoman, Inez Lord of Rollingdam, to whom they paid an honorarium. Inez succeeded her mother, Helen (Murphy) Reed as forewoman. Weavers dropped off "webs" of cloth, continuous lengths twenty-five- to thirty-five-yards long, in a shed attached to Inez's house where they could also collect the next warp. Inez delivered the webs to St. Andrews and brought back the money for the crafters. Later, in the 1960s, when nearly all the weavers had their own vehicles, most came directly to St. Andrews. They liked the outing.

For the crafters, the work was now year-round, although more intense in winter as they prepared for the season in St. Andrews and for spring orders from retailers. As farming declined, most were no longer farm wives, but they were still countrywomen. For the weavers, the work was also more varied. Nell's stock-in-trade had been the heavier homespun cloth, suitable for blankets, car robes, and knee rugs, but for tailored goods such as skirts and sports jackets, a lighter fabric was needed. A boxed sweater set, a skirt length of fabric with matching yarn for a pullover or cardigan, became Cottage Craft's best known item. The fabric for sports jackets was sent to Montreal for tailoring. All the coats, skirts, and embroidered jackets, however,

were made by a tailor in town. Ida Kline did the embroidery for
the jackets. Celebrities who came to town for a few days or for the
season often became ambassadors for Cottage Craft goods. When
Lady Dunn, the wife of steel magnate Sir James Dunn, opened the
Lady Dunn auditorium at the St. Andrews Community College, she
wore a Cottage Craft outfit: a jacket, skirt, sweater, and a pill-box
hat. Ida Kline did the embroidery for the entire outfit. The skater
Barbara Ann Scott donned a Cottage Craft toque and left with a tar-
tan designed by Bon Harriot, and on their visit to mark St. Andrews'
bicentennial, in 1983, Prince Charles and Princess Diana were presented with matching Cottage Craft sweaters for themselves and with
a handmade tweed frog for the young Prince William.

In their efforts to broaden the market, the Ross brothers also added new colours and extended the range of small goods. This ran from
woven and embroidered bags, dolls, toques, embroidered gauntlet
style gloves, and mittens to stuffed animals (squirrels, lobsters, rab-
bits, frogs, stuffed with moss or scrap tweed and yarn). "A whole pile
of them would come in," Basil Lowery recalled, "and within a week
they'd be gone." Kent Ross painted the faces of some of the dolls.
The new colours, among them Blue Spruce and Fundy Fog, were
used in both knitted and woven tweed goods. After Acker's time, the
homespun fabric came to Cottage Craft in fifty-yard lengths. It was
then washed in the washer, the two ends having been sewn together so
an impossible tangle didn't develop. After washing, the moisture was
removed with an extractor, the fabric wound onto a tube and when
still damp taken to the Charlotte County Laundry in St. Andrews to
be pressed.

A two- to threefold increase in output required a greater, as well as
a steady, supply of yarn. Under Nell, Cottage Craft yarn had been spun
by the Speedy Mill in St. Stephen from wool she had bought locally
and dyed at Beech Hill. But shortly after the Rosses' accession, the
Speedy Mill changed hands and a contretemps with the new owners
prompted Kent and Bill Ross to look elsewhere. For locally spun wool
there were three choices: a mill at Golden Grove, on the far side of
Saint John; another at Woodstock; and another, the Briggs and Little

Mill at Harvey, just beyond the halfway point between St. Andrews and Fredericton. In premotoring days, when sheep were plentiful, there used to be a mill every forty or fifty miles, a day's travel by horse. The Briggs and Little Mill, the most convenient to St. Andrews and the choice of the Rosses, began working probably in the 1850s as a simple washing and carding mill, operating for part of the year after shearing. Customers then took the rovings home to spin and dye, and so on. Until the 1940s, the mill produced only cream, black, and grey yarn, adding colours after 1945 in response to demand.

A summer ritual: hooking wool skeins around a rope of cork floats.

Courtesy of Mary Janet Clift

Bill and Kent approached the owners, Roy and Ward Little, and asked if they would be able to duplicate Cottage Craft colours and do the spinning for them.

Bill and Kent came to a verbal agreement with the Littles that allowed them to use the formulae for Cottage Craft colours, which Nell had entered in a small notebook, as long as they didn't cut into Cottage Craft's market. Over the past fifty years or so the two different colour ranges have merged so that neither is exclusive any longer. When necessary, each business can call on the other's inventory to some extent. According to John Little, the current co-owner and sales manager of the mill, "Kent was like a computer before there were computers." He always kept meticulous records of quantities and colours and sizes of yarns bought in a given year and gauged what they needed to order for the following year.

Briggs and Little still buy all available and suitable wool from local producers but as local production has declined, they have been forced to look farther afield — to Nova Scotia, Prince Edward Island, Quebec, and Newfoundland. The balance of their needs they buy from Canadian Cooperative Wool in Carleton Place, Ontario, which buys wool from all over Canada. Sheep raising in New Brunswick, and in Canada in general, was hit hard by the decision of the New Zealand government to supply fresh lamb by jet plane all around the world only twenty-four hours after slaughter. In the Maritimes, wool was always a by-product; sheep and lambs were raised for their meat and the arrival of cheaper New Zealand lamb saw a swift decline in numbers.

The spun yarn came to Cottage Craft, in five-pound bales of one ply or two ply, in a large truck from Harvey. The parcels, wrapped in brown kraft paper, were tossed or passed up through large loft doors to the second floor. Weaving yarn came on cones. Each weaver got a full setting, thirty cones of warp and thirty cones of weft to produce sixty yards of fabric. The main yarn delivery was usually in late spring and was enough to see the store through the summer retail business and to satisfy the fall demand from outlying knitters and weavers for yarn for their winter production. Today, deliveries are made year-round, as the mill, because of the merging of colours and yarns, works on its own production and Cottage Craft production simultaneously. When John Little worked in the mill's shipping department as a young man, he delivered the spring order and would often be invited out to Kent's camp for a lobster feed and drinks. It made for a late trip home. The Rosses, he added, "enjoyed life."

In 1980, Kent suffered a stroke, at the age of fifty-eight. A year or two earlier, he had bought out Bill's half of the business. Bill wanted to retire. Kent had another stroke in the summer of 1983, but it didn't prevent him from going, in a wheelchair, from his floor of the Saint John Regional hospital to see Rita Greenlaw who was on another having surgery for cancer. While Kent was in hospital, Rita, Ida Kline, and Dot Alexander, the secretary, sent him a card almost every day, often with a funny cartoon enclosed. Kent, Rita remarked, was "a great boss, both of them for that matter."

Kent died in 1984 at sixty-two. After his death, his widow Elizabeth Ross, a former insurance agent, and their son Jim, took over the business, and then, in 1994, Jim's brother Evan and Evan's wife, Michelle. Evan and Michelle now live in Kent and Elizabeth ('Liz') Ross's house, where Evan grew up. Built in 1825, the house on King Street retains all of its essential colonial features: a generous central hallway and staircase, well-proportioned rooms to each side, small-paned windows, pine floors, mantels, fireplaces, and a magnificent open hearth. Even the telephone number, Evan notes, hasn't changed since he was a boy. Near the beginning of Evan and Michelle's tenure at Cottage Craft, fire destroyed the Briggs and Little Mill in Harvey, precipitating a crisis. They tried using wool from Alberta, but it was of such poor quality that the knitters and weavers complained. Luckily, there was a stockpile of yarn and bolts of tweed that they eked out carefully over the next three years. To add value to it, they had it made up into finished items rather than selling it as yarn or as lengths of tweed. When Briggs and Little started production again in 1997, Cottage Craft was down to forty skeins of pink wool. "All our sweaters" they remark, "were Briar Rose by the end of it."

Since the Briggs and Little fire and the hiatus in the local production of yarn, the pool of knitters, now up to 150, encompasses the whole of the Maritimes and Newfoundland. There are also a handful from Ontario and Alberta, most of them Maritimers who moved away. In Charlotte County, there are few farms left, and many women, while still running the household, work outside the home. With a smaller catch of local knitters, the net has had to be spread wider. Whereas farm women needed the income, many of the out-workers today knit chiefly for love of the craft and, as some readily admit, for the release of stress. The only exceptions are knitters, who make up roughly one third of the whole, from the small outports of Newfoundland where jobs and money are scarce.

With less time available to them, fewer women, too, are prepared to take on time-consuming projects. Knitters for heavy hooded sweaters with complex patterns are difficult to find, as are doll and toy makers. To make the John Passa and the Marie Maquoddy dolls, Mary Bryant used stiff clothesline wire for the arms and legs, silk cloth stuffed with cotton for the heads, raw wool fleece for the hair and, if the hands were joined, also for the muffs. She hand painted the faces and knitted all the clothing. Knitters are paid by the piece, not the hour, making a project of this kind a labour of love.

Work is allotted according to the tastes and skills of the knitters. Women who prefer working with two needles make sweaters and scarves; socks, gloves, and mitts are the province of women who can work, or who prefer working, with four or even six needles. Nina Murphy, a legendary local knitter, who worked until she was 102, specialized in argyle socks whose complex ribbing and multicoloured diamond shapes required many needles and up to nine bobbins. For each of the knitters, Evan Ross decides on the product, the patterns, and the colours. The yarn, still supplied by Briggs and Little, is shipped to them. Each of the knitters has a sweater pattern book but sweaters may also be custom-made to a particular pattern, colour, and size. Evan and Michelle have expanded the colour range but they remain faithful to local names and colours. Three striking recent additions are Sage Green; St. Croix Blue, a deep navy blue; Horizon Blue, which is lighter; and Kelp, a rich seaweed green that echoes the colour of parts of the foreshore. Less striking but still appealing is a new charcoal and forest-brown tweed, made into blankets that resembles pre-industrial colours. Flecks in the tweed simulate the chaff and burdocks found in the older tweeds.

A recent boon to the business has been the renaissance in hand knitting, driven chiefly by urban professionals and celebrities. Between late December and May, when the Cottage Craft store is open for only a few days in the week, 90 percent of the business's revenue comes from mail-order sales of sweater packs and knitting yarn, chiefly to the United States. *Stitches*, the Baltimore knitting show, is an annual fixture in Evan and Michelle Ross's marketing and promotional plans. There is now a movie based on Kate Jacobs's *The Friday*

Cottage Craft today. Courtesy of Matthew Rees

Night Knitting Club, a novel about the lives of a group of knitters who meet regularly at a New York wool shop. Responsive to a renewed interest in wool, a producer of the Coen brothers' movie *A Serious Man* requested for one of the characters an "Elizabeth" cardigan that he had seen on the Cottage Craft website. The "Elizabeth" cardigan, made with a cable pattern from lightweight single-ply wool, is named for Liz Ross (née Mallory), Evan's mother.

Changes in fashion and design, and the reduced leisure time available to working women, has seen a decline in demand for boxed skirt and sweaters sets, once a mainstay of the business. Skirt lengths and matching yarn are still sold but only on demand. Working women tend to prefer cardigans, which are easier to put on and take off, and fewer women now sew. Many communities, too, lack professional seamstresses and tailors. St. Andrews, which until the 1980s had three professional tailors, now has only one. A single weaver, Noella Black, from the Rollingdam district north of St. Andrews, now supplies the demand for homespun, or woven fabric. Noella is the daughter of weavers Warren and Ivy Payne, who both wove for Cottage Craft.

Warren was a woodsman who wove part-time, weaving perhaps ten yards in the early morning before going to work at a moveable lumber mill. He learned to weave from his wife Ivy, while recovering from an injury to his hand. Noella weaves on her mother's loom in an extension to her house built for the purpose by her husband Eugene Black, who is also a woodsman. She began weaving when she was twelve or thirteen, her mother having forbidden her and her two sisters to earn extra cash by picking blueberries, which was considered too hard on the back. Noella, who aims to produce ten yards a day, weaves to Evan Ross's specifications; Evan supplies the yarn and stipulates the colour and the pattern. The woven fabric is then cut and made up into blankets, car robes, and knee rugs. The waste is used for making toys, dolls, and braided rugs. When working, Noella Black wears no watch or stone-mounted rings because the constant jarring from the beater, the tool that pushes the weft firmly into place, ruins them. Electric lights attached to the loom also have a short lifespan. The yarn is still oily from the oil added for the spinning, so Noella wears old clothes and doesn't wash them until she has finished the forty-yard web. Nor, when weaving, does she vacuum the house; the wool might be oily but dust and lint still fly through it.

A recent addition to the inventory is tweed handbags, made from handwoven tweed and leather, and tailored in Montreal by a Canadian manufacturer. Tweed sport coats, ladies jackets, and trench coats may, after a spell in the fashion wilderness, once again return to the inventory. Despite periodic downturns in the demand for wool and handmade goods, the Rosses have resisted the temptation to move any of their production offshore. Except for the washing and pressing of the fabric, now done in a local laundromat rather than in-house, the methods of production are unchanged. Nell Mowat would approve.

Epilogue

Retirement left Nell, a still energetic seventy-year-old, free to indulge her interests in painting, sketching, and writing. She painted landscapes and still lifes and made her own Christmas cards. In 1951, she completed the novel *Broken Barrier* that she had been working on intermittently for ten years. The novel, about a young woman who leaves her family's farm on the St. John River to find work in New York, is based in part on the pattern of her own life. But Nell was no novelist. The plot hung on a series of improbable coincidences. An attempt to convert the novel into a play met with rejection. Raphail Kelly, head of the Canadian Repertory Theatre at the La Salle Academy, Ottawa, liked the farm scenes, when the play "came to life," but he found the plot slow moving and the characterization unconvincing.

The work is memorable chiefly for the expression of Nell's likes and dislikes, her "little sermons," as Mary Gove Carson might have said. The farm lands and the farm life of the St. John River received high praise, as did Fredericton, "a beautiful little city, set like a gem on a wide river." New York is tolerated, but Americans who think the American Revolution justified are vilified. George Washington was an ingrate and the maligned King George, "the most misjudged monarch in all history." She repeated her defence of George III six years later in an article, "The Tories King," published by *The Atlantic Advocate*. Her tone may have been more measured but the argument was no better balanced. As always, however, she was admirably forthright: "I am a Tory — an old Tory. Not a Tory of the present day but the kind that lived in the eighteenth century." Saul Bellow, in Nell's shoes, might have written "I am a Loyalist, New Brunswick born." The *Advocate's* editor, anxious not to offend American readers, was careful to say that Nell's views, though interesting, were controversial.

In spite of its improbable plot and unconvincing characters, the novel managed to find a publisher. *Broken Barrier* was the maiden publication of the University Press of New Brunswick. Lieutenant Governor D. L. McLaren wrote a foreword and the novel was serialized in Fredericton's *Daily Gleaner*. As a romance, it did not receive serious critical attention. Notices in the provincial press were little more than plot summaries. Mary K. Hall, a bookseller in Fredericton, however, commented very favourably on a radio interview given by Nell: "I listened to your broadcast last night with a great deal of pleasure. It was original, interesting and different from the regular run of broadcasts." She added that she would be advertising the book in the *Gleaner* the following Saturday and hoped to do well with it. Nell also received letters of congratulation from Kenneth Sills, president of Bowdoin College, who owned a house in St. Andrews, and from Esther Clark Wright, historian and author (amongst other works) of a seminal history of the New Brunswick Loyalists. Kenneth Sills described the novel as "a very pretty story, well told," and marvelled at the way in which she and other authors handled dialogue. Esther Clark Wright who, at the time, was working on her Loyalist history, "an endless job," found Nell's book interesting and carefully worked out and was delighted that Nell had found a publisher.

Even without the publication of *Broken Barrier*, 1951 would have been a signal year for Nell. At a meeting in Fredericton with senior academics of the University of New Brunswick early in 1951, Lord Beaverbrook, who was then the chancellor of the university, raised the subject of an honorary degree for Grace Helen Mowat. He did so at the suggestion of his lifelong friend Sir James Dunn, president

Nell at her desk at Beech Hill, circa 1960.
Courtesy of the Charlotte County Archives

of Algoma Steel, who had lived in St. Andrews since 1947. The university president, Bud Trueman, replied that the list of recipients had already been published, and that it would be extremely awkward to add another name, however deserving of an honorary doctorate Nell might be. Lord Beaverbrook remained adamant, however, and Bud Truman appended Nell's name to the list. She was driven to the degree ceremony by Bill and Kent Ross. On the journey home, she sat back, lit a cigarette, and said to the brothers in tones that probably mingled self-satisfaction with impish delight at having scaled a major academic height: "I guess I'm becoming famous by degrees." It may have been her last recorded witticism. Nell Mowat died at Beech Hill in her ninetieth year, in February 1964.

Selected Bibliography

UNPUBLISHED SOURCES

Grace Helen Mowat Collection. Charlotte County Archives, St. Andrews, NB.

Rygeil, Judith Anne. "Women of the Cloth, Weavers in Westmorland and Charlotte Counties, New Brunswick 1871-1897." PhD thesis, Carleton University, 1998.

Sackett, Andrew J. "Doing history in the 'Great Cyclorama of God:' Tourism and the Presentation of the Past in Twentieth-Century St. Andrews, New Brunswick." MA thesis, Queen's University, 1995.

Wren, Frances. "Recollections of My Work with Dr. Grace Helen Mowat." *Proceedings of the Charlotte County Historical Society*, vol. 6, 1971. Reprinted in the *St. Croix Courier*, February 7, 1979.

NEWSPAPERS

The Saint John Telegraph-Journal, 1922-1963.

The St. Andrews Bay Pilot, 1885-1888.

The St. Andrews Beacon, 1893-1919.

The St. Andrews Standard, 1873.

The St. Croix Courier, 1920-1979.

OTHER WORKS

Albee, Helen R. *Abnakee Rugs*. Cambridge: Riverside Press, 1903.

Cooper Union. Annual Reports of the Woman's Art School. 1897-1900.

Cunningham, Lewis Arthur. "Among the Cottage Crafters." *Canadian Home Journal*, March 1933.

Jack, David Russell. "The Mowat Family." *Acadiensis*, vol. 8, no. 4 (October 1908).

Mowat, Grace Helen. *A Story of Cottage Craft*. St. Andrews: Charlotte County Cottage Craft, 1958.

———. "Art as a Cash Crop." *Dalhousie Review*, vol. 22, no.1 (April 1942).

———. *Broken Barrier*. Fredericton: University Press of New Brunswick, 1951.

———. *Funny Fables of Fundy and Other Poems for Children* Ottawa: Ru-Mi-Lou Books, 1928.

———. *The Diverting History of A Loyalist Town: A Portrait of St, Andrews, New Brunswick*. Fredericton: Brunswick Press, 1953.

———. "The Tories:' King George III and the Seeds of the Revolution." *The Atlantic Advocate*, vol. 48 (October 1957). Reprinted by the Charlotte County Historical Society, 1976.

Pringle, Gertrude E.S. "Back to the Days of Cottage Craft: The Story of Helen G. Mowat and How She Succeeded in Expanding $10 to $12,000." *Maclean's*, March 1, 1922.

———. "Where Cottage Craft is Plied." *Modern Priscilla*, February 1923.

Rankin, Norman S. "Bringing Playtime to the Farm." *Maclean's*, October 15, 1924.

Ross, Victoria Burrill. *Moments Make a Year*. Sackville N.B.: Tribune Press, 1926.

Sackett, Andrew J. "Inhaling the Salubrious Air: Health and Development in St. Andrews, NB, 1880-1910." *Acadiensis*, vol 25, no.1 (Autumn 1995).

Sclanders, Ian. "The Famous Cottage Craft Industry Founded and Directed in Charlotte County by Miss Grace Helen Mowat." *Saint John Telegraph-Journal*, November 10, 1937.

————. "The St. Andrews Weavers." *Saint John Telegraph-Journal*, March 5, 1949.

Walker, Willa. *No Hay Fever and a Railway: Summers in St. Andrews, Canada's First Seaside Resort*. Fredericton: Goose Lane Editions, 1989.

Photo Credits

The images on pages 2, 16, 19, 21, 23, 25, 45, 69, 73, 78, 83, 85, 86, 96, 101, 115, 132, 133, 144, 155, 159, 163, 181, 182, 184, 187, 190, and 203 and the letter on page 123 appear courtesy of the Charlotte County Archives.

The photos on pages 12 and 199 appear courtesy of Matthew Rees.

The photo on page 31 appears courtesy of *The Listener*.

The photos and other illustrative material on pages 41, 134, 135, 138, 140, 141, 149, and 162 appear courtesy of the Ross Memorial Museum, St. Andrews.

The photos on pages 48 and 53 appear courtesy of Greg Cohane.

The photos on pages 57, 93, 95, and 179 appear courtesy of Anthony E. Hilditch.

One of the photos on page 129 appears courtesy of M. Aileen Smith.

One of the photos on page 129 and the photos on page 143 appear courtesy of Sheila Simpson.

The photos on pages 130, 131, 166, and 224 appear courtesy of Rev. Dr. Basil Lowery.

One of the photos on page 132 and on page 140 appear courtesy of Andrew Leighton.

209

One of the photos on page 133 appears courtesy of Bunny Campbell.

One of the photos on page 134 and on page 135, both of the photos on page 136, and one of the photos on page 142 appear courtesy of the late E.B. Ross and Elizabeth Ross.

The photos on pages 137, two of the photos on page 138, all of the photos on page 139, and one of the photos on page 142 appear courtesy of Cottage Craft.

One of the photos on page 141 appears courtesy of the Sir James Dunn Academy, St. Andrews.

One of the photos on page 144 and the photo on page 195 appear courtesy of Mary Janet Clift.

The photo of Bliss Carman on page 169 is from the Rufus Hathaway Photograph Collection and appears courtesy of the Archives and Special Collections, Harriet Irving Library, University of New Brunswick.

The images on pages 175 and 178 are representations taken from Grace Helen Mowat. *Funny Fables of Fundy*. St. Stephen, N.B.: Blue Heron Printing Co. Ltd., 1990.

Index

211